GILDA'S
DISEASE

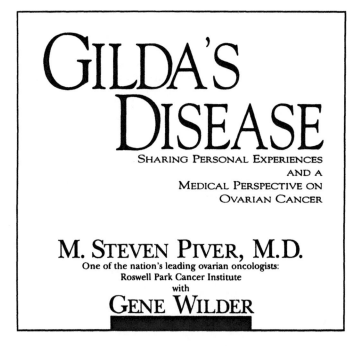

GILDA'S DISEASE

SHARING PERSONAL EXPERIENCES
AND A
MEDICAL PERSPECTIVE ON
OVARIAN CANCER

M. STEVEN PIVER, M.D.
One of the nation's leading ovarian oncologists:
Roswell Park Cancer Institute
with
GENE WILDER

BROADWAY BOOKS

NEW YORK

BROADWAY

Library of Congress Cataloging-in-Publication Data

Piver, M. Steven.
   Gilda's disease : sharing personal experiences and a
  medical perspective on ovarian cancer / M. Steven Piver
  with Gene Wilder.
     p. cm.
    Originally published: Amherst, N.Y. : Prometheus Books,   1996.
    Includes bibliographical references (p.) and index.
    ISBN 0-7679-0138-X (pbk.)
    1. Ovaries—Cancer—Popular works. I. Wilder, Gene,
  1935– .
  II. Title.
  RC280.08P576   1998
  616.99'465—dc21   97-45517
                                           CIP
  LSI 001

To all the other Gildas

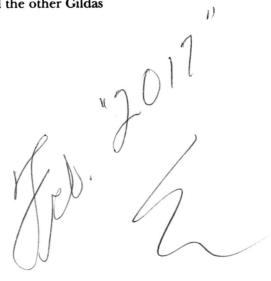

Acknowledgments

To the two people who went over every word, comma, and semi-colon—Debra Piver and Cheryl Blake—our heartfelt appreciation and thanks!

A special thanks to our editor, Steven L. Mitchell, for his continued enthusiasm for this book as the different parts came together, and to Associate Editor Eugene O'Connor, for respecting our wishes during the important editing process.

This book is not meant to be a substitute for a discussion with a physician. Rather, we hope it is a help during those times. Finally, with medicine changing so rapidly, some of the information might become outdated.

Contents

Figures

Foreword

Joanna Bull

To read *Gilda's Disease* is to be lucky enough to walk into a new room and be introduced to a rare collection of people you'd never ordinarily meet. What's unusual about these people is that they all want you to learn everything useful that you could possibly want to know about ovarian cancer. If you're dealing with ovarian cancer now or have it in your family, these are true friends.

Gilda herself will tell you directly about some of her experiences, many of which you may recognize as your own. Thanks to her generosity and openness, you might be able to learn from her "surprises" and avoid some of them yourself. While you're reading *Gilda's Disease*, here's hoping that something of Gilda's endless supply of humor in the face of the unknown will rub off on you. She had plenty to share, and it never left her. You'll also learn from her courage, but you probably already have a store of that, or you wouldn't be reading this book.

Dr. Steve Piver will introduce himself to you and provide easy, friendly access to medical information and advice about the particulars of ovarian cancer. He will shed light on the complexities of this disease (Did you know that there are *thirty* kinds of ovarian cancer?) so that you won't feel in the dark anymore about its salient features, the ones that matter to you. Causes and prevention, symptoms and the difficulties of diagnosis, staging and treatment options, including "alternatives," are all beamed in on by one of the most comprehensive minds in the field of ovarian cancer. All this, and he's the kind of doctor who personally comes to the telephone, if he can, when you call.

Gene Wilder is here, sharing the too common saga of Mr. and Mrs. Gene Wilder's search for an explanation of Gilda's symptoms, a search that finally led to ovarian cancer—which had, tragically, been there all along. Gene Wilder's oversized heart is so constituted that he must always search further, for the meaning that's hidden in confusion. He found it in "Gilda's great gift" to him and to us. Gene's advice for husbands and significant others can be extended to all human beings who are reminded through illness that we are mortal and *it is that very fact* that gives each minute of our living its preciousness.

Finally, you'll meet a number of women who have written Dr. Piver and Gene Wilder, women who wanted to share their stories and say thanks for putting the word out about ovarian cancer. Courage has been defined as proceeding with confidence even when you're really scared and don't know at all where you'll actually wind up. These women have such courage in abundance. Their confidence comes from knowledge, information, thoughtful action, a sense of partnership with their health care teams, and hope. Why not hope? Statistics exist, but you're so much more than a statistic. When you don't know the outcome of something, all endings are possible. That's a kind of freedom.

There are a few people missing from this room; you'll find them at Gilda's Club, now open in New York City with branches in development throughout the nation. *Gilda's Disease* looks at ovarian cancer from all perspectives save that of its missing piece—and that of all cancers: *emotional and social support* when facing this illness. It's to Steve Piver's eternal credit that by inviting you to meet Gilda's Club in this foreword he is reminding you that such support is an essential ingredient in the total treatment picture. (Gilda's Club, co-founded by Gene Wilder and myself and countless generous friends, is without charge, which makes Steve's generosity in sharing revenues from this book especially appreciated. This is one good guy.)

Gilda once said that having cancer gave her membership in an elite club that she'd rather not belong to. In Gilda's honor, we invite you to come on by the clubhouse, whatever your type of cancer, whether family or friends, adults or kids. Get the best medical care you can find, and then "join the club"—set up a structured program for living with cancer that has goals as clear as those of chemotherapy or radiation or surgery. At Gilda's Club, you'll learn how from the "experts" who've been there and are going through it with you. We're open in New York and will soon be operating in Detroit, Michigan, and south Florida. North Coast, Ohio; Nashville, Tennessee; Toronto, Ontario; Seattle, Washington; Boise, Idaho; and Burlington, Vermont, have all given permission to start raising funds for clubhouses in their areas.

Back to our room. Walk into it with confidence. Learn. Expand your resources. Enjoy your new friends. Eat a strawberry, even though the tigers may be snarling. It tastes so sweet right now.

Introduction

M. Steven Piver, M.D.

I'm not sure whether other authors, like me, write their introductions last. Conventional form notwithstanding, I'm particularly pleased that I followed this formula because, after reading a draft of the book, my daughter Debra wrote that it would help *women and their families feel less scared, less alone,* when faced with ovarian cancer.

Gilda's Disease is about more than comedienne Gilda Radner's unsuccessful battle with ovarian cancer.

In a sense, this book is about love. About people who knew and loved Gilda and thousands upon thousands of people who never knew her, but also loved her. It is about trying (with the emphasis on trying) to make what is known about ovarian cancer accessible to a wider audience. It is clear to me that everyone, both those who knew her and those, like me, who never met her but thought they knew her, believed that Gilda was so accessible, so easy to approach. So much so that we all felt that we knew her intimately.

This book is also about communication. I learned about Gilda's deep belief in the power of communication in her autobiography, *It's Always Something*. In it she wrote: "If indeed God created the world and left us on our own to work things out, then getting together with other people to communicate is what we should be doing."

Back to the beginning. Gilda Radner died of ovarian cancer on May 20, 1989. Ten days later, Sally Squires, a reporter for the *Washington Post*, wrote an article titled "Fighting Ovarian Cancer—Doctors Don't Know Who's at Risk, or Why?" She stated:

> Genetics could also play a role in a very small number of cases. At Roswell Park Cancer Institute in Buffalo, M. Steven Piver has collected a national Registry of 200 ovarian cancer families where the disease reappears in each generation. Piver said that the risk of developing ovarian cancer is one in 70 or about 1.4 percent for the average American woman, but if two or more first-degree relatives have it, you have a 50 percent chance of developing ovarian cancer and that for this reason, doctors now recommend that women with a family history of ovarian cancer have their ovaries prophylactically removed at age 35.

For the first time ever, ovarian cancer had *come out of the closet* because of who Gilda Radner was and what she meant to so many people. Apparently, the days of no newspaper or magazine articles or television specials on ovarian cancer were over.

Seven weeks later, July 25, 1989, Larry Altman, a medical writer for the *New York Times*, wrote an article titled "Research Links Diet and Infertility Factors to Ovarian Cancer." Actor Gene Wilder, Gilda's husband, read the article and wrote Altman to ask why he hadn't mentioned anything about the blood test CA125 (see pp. 70, 73) in diagnosing ovarian cancer and the family link to the disease. Larry Altman suggested that Gene may want "to speak to Steven Piver in Buffalo, New York."

Gene called. And ever since that telephone call brought together the actor from Milwaukee, with his unanswered questions on ovarian cancer, and the cancer surgeon from Buffalo, we have combined our efforts to communicate some of what is known on ovarian cancer to the general public. Gene made a television public service announcement titled "Please Don't Be Afraid, Just Do It" and the Registry set up a 1–800–OVARIAN hotline. Literally tens of thousands of telephone calls (27,000 the first month) were received from people around the country asking questions about ovarian cancer.

Now, seven years later, it seemed the right time to provide in written form the known answers to many of these questions. I asked Gene to join me in writing this book, to write what he has learned that might help others who are now in the position that he once was, and to read every word to make certain that it was not too *scary*, but accessible and informative. The wonders of the fax machine made this not only doable, but rewarding for both of us. After seeing the first drafts with their many tables and figures (that's how doctors write), Gene replied, "I *urge* you to put them in an appendix." Most of the tables and figures now comfortably reside in the appendix at the end of the book.

This book is also about sharing. It's one thing to hear people say how funny Gilda was, but quite another to read what they wrote about her after she died. The Registry received hundreds of letters. Most were addressed to Gene Wilder in care of the Registry. They were from people who loved Gilda but were so saddened by her death that they wanted a vehicle to express their love. The Registry was the only address they knew. Having read all of these before sending them to Gene, I wanted to share them. Gene agreed. The letter from E. A. S. says it all.

Dear Mr. Wilder:

When I first heard of her cancer, I was deeply troubled and struck with great anguish as I thought—Why Gilda? This woman who has given so much through her acting, for so many years—and now—struck with one of the most devastating diseases on earth—she is fighting for her life. Like you, I thought her strength, will and determination would pull her through.

I share your anger and frustration, Gene, but in a different way. Just as you are trying to make a difference for the Gildas out there who still have a chance, I, too, will continue to try to make a difference for Gildas and Genes out there who are together facing the inevitable ultimate surrender.

Gilda's memory will always be with me and she will continue to reach out from the screen and touch me with that unique and rare essence that only the cherished Gilda Radner had.

Beginning with chapter 2, each chapter starts with one of these letters.

This book is also about a book. In *It's Always Something*, Gilda Radner told us exactly what she was going through mentally and physically during her illness. Passages from her autobiography are used here to put in perspective some of the subjects discussed.

Finally, this book is about the importance of family and friends and support groups in helping a woman in her battle with ovarian cancer. Gilda knew this better than anyone.

"Gene came every day and sneaked Sparkle [their Yorkshire terrier] in with him. He said that if anybody was going to stop him, he would say he bought her in the gift shop and she ran on batteries. So I got to see my Sparkle.

"Gene would go shopping in Beverly Hills and bring me beautiful things in boxes like you would see in the old movies, with big bows on them that you could take off with one pull—like Tiffany's. I'd just pull the string and the bow would come open and in the box would be a new nightgown or a new robe. It was joyful every time he appeared in the doorway bringing gifts and messages from the outside world. Gene became funnier than I have ever seen him. He is very funny in the movies but he's not that funny in real life. He's shy. He's a comic actor as opposed to a comedian. I think I am a comedienne—a performer, an entertainer, where he is an actor. But he became very funny, telling stories around my bed, assisting the nurses like Dr. Frankenstein, holding a flashlight for intricate procedures and shaking it on purpose like he was nervous.

"I became mischievous myself. I liked walking as fast as I could while Gene was pushing my IV stand, so he couldn't keep up with me. That would make me laugh so hard. It was dumb stuff, but it would make me laugh that I could walk faster than he could push my IV bottle. The nurse couldn't keep up with me either. The truth was, they were putting me on. Anyone could have gone faster than me. But I was just like a child. I felt like Eloise, the fictional little girl in the Plaza Hotel in New York. Gene would have his dinner in the hospital with me every night. I didn't eat for a month, but after he ate he'd lie in bed with me and we'd talk or watch TV. I would cry as easily as I'd laugh." (*It's Always Something*, pp. 79–80)

Gilda's first and main support group person was Joanna Bull:

"Late one afternoon, not quite two weeks after my surgery, I had my first appointment with Joanna Bull. Joanna was in her late forties. Her face was round and open and her blond hair was cut in a Buster Brown style. It was as though an angel had walked into my hospital room, an angel filled with life. I never saw anybody like her; I never saw anybody with so much spirit. She flew into the room, plopped herself fearlessly at the foot of my bed and put her arms on my legs so that there was a physical contact between us. She talked to me about cancer. She was a psychotherapist who worked at a place called The Wellness Community, where she was assistant director. She counseled cancer patients all the time, and she was just sparkly. I remember her sparkling eyes. We talked about cancer, specifically about my feelings about it. I told her that I thought this ordeal was a school I was going through, that I was meant to teach and help others. She said it was more important to see this as an 'exquisite' time to take care of myself and heal my own body. . . .

"Joanna said to me that in a way it didn't matter what happened because I had learned to live with cancer. I had learned that life goes on and you can still feel well and accomplish things, and that I really had nothing to be scared of because I knew, even with cancer, life would go on anyway. It was true. In the last six months my life hadn't stopped. I certainly had days when I didn't feel well, but I also had as many days of joy when I accomplished things—met with old friends, made new friends, rediscovered sex and life with my husband, began writing my book, started managing my home and career again. It wasn't easy. It required a lot of inner strength, and a lot of support. I had to use my imagination to get through it. The most important thing was what I learned from Joanna, not to let my life stop while I was battling cancer. Lots happened that was fun and wonderful while I was in treatment. I laughed and saw movies and read. My life didn't stop. If I had to go through chemotherapy again, I would, because it's an investment in the future. I invested ten days of yuck to get ten good days and then to get forty, fifty, or sixty years of life. That was what I wanted.

"If there were more cancer, I could handle it, but boy, would I be pissed off." (*It's Always Something*, pp. 80–81, 181–82)

It is our hope that this portrait of Gilda's courage and Gene's dedication, along with the facts presented on ovarian cancer, will help other *Gildas* and *Genes* face this disease with the same determination, but with *less* fear and with the knowledge that *they are not alone.*

All royalties from this book will benefit two organizations formed in Gilda's honor and memory. Gilda's Club (soon to be clubs) is a free, nonresidential social support community for people with cancer, their families, and friends in New York City. The Gilda Radner Familial Ovarian Cancer Registry in Buffalo, New York, tracks women with a strong family history of ovarian cancer and advises family members of their risk for developing the disease and methods of prevention. We think that Gilda would be happy with these two choices.

Chapter 1

Gilda Radner: A Personal Perspective

Gene Wilder

It's difficult to say exactly, but I think it started for Gilda during *Haunted Honeymoon,* the movie we were filming in London in September of 1985, just one year after we were married. Gilda thought she was getting the flu, but it never came. No temperature, just the "feeling," which would come and go during the next month. We didn't think of it as anything extraordinary, considering that she had had a miscarriage the month before and that it was now almost the end of autumn. England was very cold and damp that November. When our work was finished we flew happily to the sun in California.

As we were driving on our way to play tennis, on the first Sunday of January 1986, Gilda suddenly felt a wave of tiredness come over her, "like fog rolling in," she said. It lasted forty-five minutes; then she felt fine again. But she was curious.

The next day she saw a specialist in internal medicine who did a complete blood workup. "For whatever it's worth, you have something called Epstein-Barr virus. I don't even know if there is such a thing, but you've got it. Whatever it is, it's not life-threatening, so go about your business and it'll go away."

The next few weeks she ran a low-grade fever. The internist said to take aspirin or Tylenol; it helped a little.

In February she felt fine for about ten days, and then—around her menstrual cycle—the severe fatigue came back. And just when she thought a pattern was developing, it would change. At one point she stayed in bed for three days. It was starting to scare her. She saw the doctor again and he said that, in his opinion, it was emotional: because she had had the miscarriage six months earlier she was probably undergoing a depression now . . . "but nothing life-threatening!"

In March we left California and went to Gilda's home in Connecticut. The "fog" rolled in again.

In April she had pelvic cramping, so she made an appointment with a Connecticut gynecologist who did a blood test: "Absolutely nothing wrong." She sighed in relief.

In June we went to Paris. I took her to my favorite bistro and, knowing how she loved food, I was waiting for the look of ecstasy as the 'Liver with Raisins' was served. She barely ate. Walking towards the rue de Rivoli to find a taxi, she suddenly sat down on the curb, doubled over in pain as she held her stomach.

We went back to Connecticut, hoping . . . maybe all the travel, the time change, the altitudes . . . ? Her clothes started to feel tight. Things just didn't fit anymore. She had to leave the little button at the top of her pants unbuttoned. She thought it was gas.

She went to a gastroenterologist in New York who said, after an examination, "You're a very talented, very high-strung young woman. You've got to relax!" He told her to stop taking the vitamin C that she was taking in large doses (her own idea). He believed that the vitamin C might be causing all the pains in her stomach. It sounded logical and we were both relieved.

In August, she began to have shooting pains down her thighs. They would come and go. She went to New York for a sonogram. It showed some congestion, the ovaries weren't quite where they were supposed to be, but no sign of tumor, no sign of obstruction. She had a lower GI; all the pictures were normal . . . but she couldn't keep her legs still. She said that if she didn't keep moving her legs she would pull her hair out. Then she started getting thinner, although she didn't have any perceivable lack of appetite.

On the fifteenth of September, feeling that she was going crazy, with no one quite believing her, she went to Boston to see a specialist on Epstein-Barr virus. "What are you afraid of, Gilda?" "I'm afraid I have cancer." He told her that every symptom that she presented was consistent with what other patients had told him who had the Epstein-Barr virus. "Keep having blood work done. Regularly!" We went back to California.

On September 22, the internal medicine doctor in California did another blood workup. "Normal!" He recommended that she see a new gynecologist. The new doctor gave her a pelvic exam. "Normal!" Gilda was getting desperate.

She went to an acupuncturist (her idea). She said he was kind to her. (Everyone was kind to her.) The pains in her legs kept her from sleeping; her bowels stopped working regularly; her stomach blew up like a balloon. She went to a holistic doctor. He put metal devices on her pulse joints, gave her protein supplements and suggested coffee enemas. It all sounded like some medieval torture to me, but at this point, with all the doctors saying it was "nothing life-threatening" I didn't want to discourage her from trying anything that she thought might help.

On October 14, after another examination, the internist said, "You are literally full of shit, and I don't know why you're blocked up. There doesn't seem to be any reason for it." Now *he* was nervous.

On October 17, she went to the holistic doctor again and he gave her a colonic, hoping to flush out whatever might be blocking her colon. The only thing that floated out was a bean sprout.

On October 23, 1986, the internist checked her into the hospital. He decided to have fluid drawn from her abdomen. Gilda said, "At last somebody believes me." That Friday night we were told that she had ovarian cancer, stage IV. She was operated on Sunday morning. They took out a mass the size of a grapefruit. She had thirty-two hundred cc of fluid in her abdomen. She responded very well to chemotherapy and for a while the doctors were optimistic that she was going to be one of the lucky ones. But she wasn't. After two and a half years of chemotherapy; after radiation of her entire abdomen, which caused her intestines to shrivel and reject any food that tried to pass through; after four operations and an ileostomy and portable toilets and green bile and intravenous feeding all night . . . after all that, she still struggled to push everyone away, climb off the gurney and run out of the hospital on the day before she died, as she railed, "I gotta get outta here—I gotta get out—just let me out," even as doctor and nurse and orderly and husband tried to calm her. But she wouldn't look anyone in the eye. She just kept pleading, "I know, but just let me out—I got to get outta here." She left this earth on May 20, 1989.

I don't know what cancer is . . . cells gone mad, I suppose. At that time I certainly didn't know what ovarian cancer was, and it's a lucky thing. The only real virtue I displayed in those three and a half years was the result of blind ignorance. I believed, until three weeks before she died, that Gilda would pull through. And she saw it in my eyes. She'd say, "Really? You really think so?" And I'd say, "I'll trade you life spans right now."

Many men have said to me, "I don't know if I can handle this—honestly, I just don't know," as if *they* were the ones who had ovarian cancer. But if they knew how the littlest thing can boost the morale of their partner, who might very well be living in a sweating panic, day and night, afraid to admit how truly frightened she is and how much she might long for something normal in her life, something as simple as an argument. When I finally had the courage to shout at Gilda because I was fed up to the bursting point over some unjust act of hers, Gilda started crying, "Thank you, thank you, honey. I know you wouldn't argue with me if you thought I was dying. See? . . . It's good to have a fight. It's nice! Now I feel normal again."

This is what I learned from Gilda: Maybe you have another fifty years to live, maybe only fifty days. I honestly don't know if I'll be alive tomorrow. So squeeze the beauty out of every day, every moment of life, because none of us knows how long we're going to live. Isn't it ironic that happiness and suffering seem to be the only two teachers who can get that message past our brains and into our hearts?

When I was a little boy you didn't say the word "cancer" out loud. If you had to use that word, you whispered it. Gilda was worried about getting cancer from the time I met her. She used to wear an apron that had an "ANTI-CANCER DIET" printed on it. She made jokes about cancer almost every day of her life, I think in the hope that if she joked about it and said it out loud often enough, God would say, "Well, I certainly can't give it to her *now!*"

This was in the early days, when she still thought that God might be the one who dished it out. I know how difficult it is not to succumb to that particular superstition. The first thought that Gilda had, when she was told that she had cancer, was that God had deserted her. But when 'hope' returned, those thoughts disappeared.

I've met people who have said, "It was something I did, and God is punishing me for it," and others who have said, "Why me? I've done nothing!" In both cases they're saying the same thing: that God brought on their cancer. Well, we believe what we believe and superstition is universal. I can't make anyone change his or her beliefs—I just wish that I could. This is what I believe: It's not God who gave you cancer; it's not because you "needed" cancer in order to learn some lesson; it's not because of your past life or your future life—it's because of GENETICS and ENVIRONMENT!

Of course, I didn't know any of this in 1986 when Gilda felt the "fog" roll in on that first Sunday in January. And I only had a vague idea of what "ovarian cancer" was. If I had known then the little that I know now I would have asked, *begged*, that the *family history*, which every doctor is trained to take, would have been explored and then explored again, until one gifted but dissatisfied doctor was struck by the irony of the *"stomach cancer"* of Gilda's grandmother and the *breast cancer* of her mother and the *ovarian cancer* of her cousin and said to himself or herself: "Maybe we should investigate Gilda's symptoms from this point of view."

But, as I say, I didn't know any of this, then. I was schooled by my mentor, Doctor M. Steven Piver of Roswell Park Memorial Institute, who suggested in one particular letter, shortly after Gilda died, that as Harrison Ford was my "sidekick" in the film *The Frisco Kid,* he (Doctor Piver) would be my sidekick and guide me through these very difficult woods.

Truth to tell, even if some doctor had made the connection in Gilda's family history, that same internist or gynecologist might not have known what to do with the information in 1986. One gynecologist, who had previously treated Gilda, wrote to me after I inquired if she had ever heard of a blood test called CA125: "CA125 is a blood test given *after* a diagnosis of ovarian cancer. Yes, I had heard of it. No, I did not give one to Gilda." (I expect that few, if any, gynecologists would have in 1986.)

But if anyone *had* given Gilda a CA125 blood test in January of 1986, when her first symptoms were consistent with stage III ovarian cancer and 80 to 90 percent of stage III patients have an elevated CA125 . . .

If Gilda had taken oral contraceptives (the pill) for the eighteen or twenty years before she tried to become pregnant, which we now know decreases the chances of getting ovarian cancer . . .

If they had diagnosed Gilda's cancer in January of 1986 instead of October. Ten months earlier . . .

"If" and "if" and "if" . . .

There is one "if" that I'm sure of: If Gilda had known of the *family link* in ovarian cancer, she would have pursued Dr. M. Steven Piver like Stanley pursued Livingston. I'm grateful that I've found him at all, so that I can help him find other Gildas and pull them out of the woods.

> "I slept
> and dreamed
> life was beauty"

I still believe that. Thanks to Gilda, I believe it now more than ever.

Chapter 2

Causes of Ovarian Cancer

Dear Mr. Wilder:

My reason for writing is to tell you how much your beautiful wife's book, *Gilda Radner—It's Always Something,* has helped me through my illness. I was so depressed and saddened by this unfortunate twist of fate. Nothing seemed to help. Not my wonderful husband or my two beautiful children. I was just going to wait to die, until I saw Gilda's book. I loved her!

There was no one funnier or more adorable than Gilda—I bet I never missed a "Saturday Night Live" while she was on it. When I found out she was ill, I cried. When she died, I prayed—for Gilda and for you! I decided to read her book.

I read it in one evening and it has completely changed my life. I read about a woman who had all the odds against her fight with so much dignity and courage. Keeping her sense of humor, yet showing her vulnerability and fear—allowing herself to continue to love.

Her book has changed my life forever. I began to play tennis and, like Gilda, there were times I couldn't return a serve, I could barely hold a tennis racquet—but I tried so hard. And I continued to fight. I now work out 1½ hours daily and I can play a fair game of tennis.

Whenever I get down, I reach for her book. I keep it next to my bed. Sometimes all I have to do is look at her picture. She was so wonderful—truly an angel and remember, angels *never die.*

She lives on in all our hearts. I truly thank God for Gilda and for you! What you are doing is wonderful. I read *People.**

Thank you for loving Gilda Radner and thank you for still caring.

F. B.

INTRODUCTION

Gilda Radner was right. *It is always something!* And, then something else! Or at least that's how it seems. Almost daily, TV, radio, and newspapers herald new scientific health hazards. Then, subsequent reports more often than not are contradictions. How can anyone be expected to sort out the real risk factors and make behavioral changes that may really be helpful? I should add here that this includes those in the medical profession.

Ovarian cancer reports are no exception. In 1989, Harvard researchers reported that women who ate yogurt or cottage cheese once a month doubled their risk of developing ovarian cancer.† This report was highlighted in a story on ovarian cancer which appeared on July 25, 1989, in the *New York Times.* Six years later, however, in 1995, researchers from the University of Washington redid the Harvard study and reported no increased risk for yogurt or cottage cheese consumption. Unfortunately, this report received much less media coverage.

---

*Gene Wilder, "Gilda Didn't Have to Die," *People,* June 3, 1991.
†See Appendix, Table 2.2: "Ovarian Cancer & Consumption of Dairy Products (The Harvard Study)."

How often a disease occurs in a specific population of people is the territory of epidemiologists—scientists who search for statistical probabilities that point to certain risk factors for life-threatening diseases. These clues are then used by you and me to modify our lifestyles to avoid these risk factors, and, hopefully, the disease. But what about the apparent contradictions we read and hear about? Dimitrios Trichopoulos, head of the Epidemiology Department at the Harvard School of Public Health, cautions that "we [epidemiologists] are fast becoming a nuisance to society. People don't take us seriously anymore, and when they do take us seriously, we may unintentionally do more harm than good." The point is that we should evaluate each of these news bulletins in terms of our health experience, our lifestyle, and our family health history.

What do we mean when we talk about factors that increase a woman's risk of ovarian cancer? First, the technical explanation, which we hear and read too often: The amount of an apparent risk is referred to as *relative risk* (sometimes referred to as *odds ratio*). What? Exactly.

In English now. *Relative risk* is simply the statistical result of a comparison of two groups. For example, researchers may choose to study a particular risk factor, let's say smoking and lung cancer. To do this, they compare the incidence of lung cancer among smokers to the incidence of lung cancer among nonsmokers. The nonsmokers are the *control group* and represent the general population. The statistical difference between the two groups is the increased risk of lung cancer related to smoking (which we now know approaches 3,000 percent). However, because all smokers do not develop lung cancer, there must be factors other than smoking that interact to eventually cause the disease.

Relative risk for ovarian cancer is approached in the same way. Although ovarian cancer is relatively uncommon, every female born in the United States has a risk of developing ovarian cancer in her lifetime of one in 55, or 1.8 percent, an increase from one in 70, or 1.4 percent, a decade ago (see Figure 2.1). Now, if a particular risk factor for ovarian cancer doubles that risk, the lifetime risk is 2×1.8 percent, or 3.6 percent.

Enough numbers and statistics. The main risk factors for ovarian cancer are: (1) the high-fat Western diet, (2) the use of talcum powder on the genital area, (3) infertility, (4) not having children, (5) the use of fertility-stimulating drugs, and (6) a family history of ovarian and/or breast cancer in a close relative. The increased risk of developing ovarian cancer from the first five risk factors is not that great. However, women who have a family history of ovarian and/or breast cancer in a close family member face a greater risk and should be sure that their physicians are aware of their history.

Regrettably, Gilda Radner had all these risk factors. Let's take a look at each one. No statistics, I promise (hope)!

THE HIGH-FAT WESTERN DIET

"Medical experts—scientists and researchers—claim that even though our genetics can predispose us to cancer, it takes the addition of other variables like environment, including what we eat and drink and breathe, to generate the disease. I had thought that I was neurotically afraid of 'the Big C.' It was certainly always around in my family. Even my astrological sign is Cancer. But I would walk out of my way to avoid passing a sign on a building that had the word *cancer* on it. The word jumped into my face from newspapers and magazines—and kept ringing in my ears after it was said. I may have been genetically predisposed to cancer, but I wonder what the variables were in my life that added to this predisposition. Why me? Since cancer is an illness in which your body is out of control, your natural instinct is to want to control it. It runs through my mind constantly: *Why did I get this?* I go from

Figure 2.1

U.S. OVARIAN CANCER 1985-1995

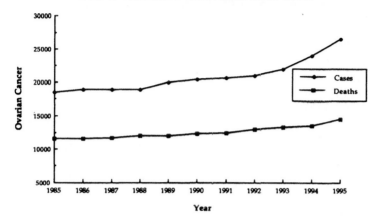

being realistic to being absurd. I wonder, *What did I do wrong? What did I do in my life that would cause this?*

"In my case, I know I used a lot of saccharin and cyclamates in my life. I would put those tablets in my coffee in the morning to make it really sweet. I had some kind of artificial sweetener that I got from Canada when they took it off the market in the U.S. because it was a suspected carcinogen. My father smuggled beer into the United States: I smuggled cyclamates. I used them in cooking and I was drinking Tab besides. I was heavy into saccharin and cyclamates for over twenty years. . . .

"I have always loved red candies. I was like a Red Dye #2 junkie. Red licorice, red jelly beans, lollipops—you name it. If there was a choice, I always ate red candies. I was packing them away all those years. Even when I heard that Red Dye #2 was carcinogenic, I still would go for them. . . .

". . . I barbecued every Memorial Day weekend in my life, every Fourth of July, every Labor Day and every Sunday in the summer. Gene loves to barbecue, too. I have heard you aren't supposed to eat burnt food—anything burnt is carcinogenic—and I love burnt stuff. These are the things that run through my head, from the sensible to the ridiculous. I ate red meat. I used hairspray." (*It's Always Something*, pp. 94–97)

We know that ovarian cancer occurs more often in middle- and upper-class women from highly industrialized countries. The only exception is Japan, which has a low, but rising, number of ovarian cancer cases. However, when Japanese women come to live in the United States, they and their daughters have an incidence of ovarian cancer approaching that of Caucasian women in the United States. Is this a coincidence? Or are there some other factors in Western countries that may be involved?

To find out, researchers chose diet as the factor to compare the two groups. Why? Because historically, the Japanese diet, which includes large quantities of rice and fish, has been characterized as low-fat, while the diet in the West, specifically the United States, has been characterized as high-fat—lots of red meat and dairy products.

Their studies showed that as the fat grams each of us consume each day increased in the United States between 1948 and 1986, so did the incidence of ovarian cancer. The same trend was occurring in Japan, particularly between 1958 and 1986 in Miyagi, Japan, where, according to a special study, the incidence of ovarian cancer doubled.

Also lending support to the connection of a high-fat diet with ovarian cancer is a 1990 report from Roswell Park Cancer Institute, in Buffalo, New York. Researchers evaluated the association between ovarian cancer and the animal fat content of milk. Women who drank only skim or 2 percent milk actually had a decreased risk of ovarian cancer. However, the risk for women who drank more than one glass of whole milk per day each tripled.*

---

*See Appendix, Table 2.1: "Ovarian Cancer and Milk Consumption: Roswell Park Cancer Institute, 1982–1988."

TALC ("BABY POWDER")

Talc has been implicated in the development of ovarian cancer because of its relationship to asbestos, a known cancer-causing agent, and its presence in many personal hygiene products. Talc particles are physically similar to asbestos and, until recently, most talc powders contained small amounts of asbestos. Talc is found in soaps, powders, deodorants, condoms, and contraceptive diaphragms. In fact, until recently, many contraceptive diaphragms and condoms were stored in talcum powder.*

The theory is that talc particles travel to the ovary through the cervix and then line the uterus and fallopian tubes, resulting in toxic effects on the ovary (see Figure 2.2). In one of the first studies on this possible link in 1982, researchers from Harvard Medical School reported that using talc or dusting powder on perineal napkins doubled a woman's risk for ovarian cancer. However, six years later (here we go again!), researchers from Stanford University could find no increased risk whether women never used talc or had used it for more than ten years.

While studies have shown that access of talc particles through the cervix to the ovaries is plausible, the role of these materials in causing ovarian cancer is unclear. What is clear is that if there is any increased risk, it's small, and may be even smaller since 1976, when manufacturers voluntarily initiated guidelines on permissible levels of asbestos in powders. However, with the significant increase in the use of condoms brought on by the AIDS epidemic, it is important to know that talcum powder is used on most condoms manufactured in the United States and abroad.†

I recognize the dilemma posed by this information. Should the possible small increased risk of ovarian cancer from presence

---

*See Appendix, Table 2.3: "Ovarian Cancer & Talc Exposure in Perineal Hygiene (The Harvard Study)."

†C. S. Kaspar and P. J. Chandler, "Possible Morbidity in Women from Talc on Condoms," *JAMA* 273 (1995): 846–47.

Figure 2.2

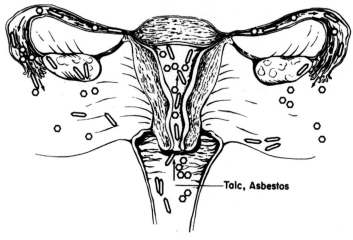

Talc, Asbestos

of talc on condoms outweigh the risks associated with AIDS by not using condoms? The answer is NO, especially if you have none of the other known risk factors for ovarian cancer.

NEVER PREGNANT, INFERTILITY

"For almost a year before my marriage, I had stopped using any form of birth control. I figured my pregnancy was another sure way to get Gene . . . but pregnancy hadn't come.

"I saw the dye running through my reproductive system on a closed-circuit screen in the examining room. There I was lying on a table with my legs spread apart watching the worst show I'd ever seen on television. The show was called 'My Tubes Were Closed.' It was about a thirty-eight-year-old newlywed who finds out she is infertile. Those tubes have to be opened for an egg to get fertilized and slide into the uterus. I remember the attending nurse looking at the screen with a long, sad face and me asking, 'What's wrong?' and her saying:

" 'Your gynecologist will explain it to you—really we can't give you the information.'

"Then her face dropped even longer. I mean, what could be lovelier than Gilda Radner and Gene Wilder having a baby? The hair alone would make people squeal with delight, but my tubes were definitely closed." (*It's Always Something*, pp. 30–31)

Sadly, Gilda Radner's infertility problems prevented her from realizing her dream of becoming pregnant and having a child. While Gilda's problems were physical, the trend among many women in highly industrialized countries is to postpone starting families until after their careers are established. This delay has resulted in a significant increase in infertility, most commonly following *endometriosis,** and less often after *pelvic inflammatory disease.*†

Although some studies have shown that ovulating women who were never pregnant and who have never used oral contraceptives increase their risk of ovarian cancer, researchers at Stanford University believe that this increased risk is related more to some unknown factor—possibly a hormone or endocrine abnormality—that leads to the inability to conceive among ovulating women who have had sexual intercourse for many years unprotected by contraception. They report that married, infertile women who failed to conceive following ten or more years of unprotected intercourse doubled their risk for ovarian cancer.‡

---

*Ectopic occurrence of endometrial tissue (lining of the uterine cavity) in the ovaries or pelvis.

†Bacterial infection of the ovaries and fallopian tubes.

‡See Appendix, Table 2.4: "Ovarian Cancer & Risk of Unprotected Intercourse (Stanford University Study)."

What's the answer? At this point, there is no definitive explanation for why women who use oral contraceptives and have multiple children have a decreased risk of ovarian cancer while those who don't have an increased risk. One theory—the excessive pituitary hormone (gonadotropin) secretion theory—holds that ovarian cancer is the result of very high levels of gonadotropin acting on the ovaries.* However, this theory is questionable because the highest blood levels of this pituitary hormone have been seen in postmenopausal women whose ovaries are no longer functioning, which is consistent with the high average age of ovarian cancer—sixty-one years.

FERTILITY DRUGS

"What happens next, in even simpler terms, is that certain hormones are injected into you daily that make your ovaries release more eggs than usual. . . .

"During the procedure, the woman can go to the hospital daily to get her daily hormone injections, but the doctors prefer that the husband give the shots so that he can feel more involved. Gene had been in the medical corps in the army and had given shots before, but I still made him practice on an orange and a grapefruit about one hundred times. He gave me my first injection in an examining room at UCLA with a nurse and doctor in the room. He was great. From then on, Gene gave me two shots a day at home." (*It's Always Something*, pp. 33–34)

---

*Pituitary gonadotropins stimulate the ovaries for follicle and corpus luteum ("yellow body") production with the production of estrogen and progesterone.

An article in the September 1994 issue of *Harpers Bazaar,* "Ovarian Cancer: One Woman's Fight. Fertility Drugs in Her Late 20s, Ovarian Cancer in Her Early 40s, If There Is a Link, *Bazaar's* Editor-in-Chief Wants to Know," began:

It all started with a missed ob/gyn appointment, just a routine feet in the stirrups, undignified probing of the private parts that she put off for a year (too busy—new job, new city, new country). But she felt vaguely lousy all last fall and when she finally went for a checkup in December, her stomach was bloated. The doctor noted on her file that she had unsuccessful treatment with the fertility drugs Clomid and Perganol in the late 1970s and ultimately adopted two children. She was immediately referred to an oncologist and within two weeks she was having surgery for ovarian cancer, stage III. At stage IV they tell you to go home and get your affairs in order. This woman is dismayed and frustrated that she was never told of an infertility drug-cancer link, that she never had a chance to evaluate the risk/benefit ratio or, after choosing treatment, to have vigilant screening. She is determined that other women be better informed, and she has the podium to carry out her mandate: this woman is Elizabeth Tilberis, the Editor-in-Chief of *Harpers Bazaar.*

Women taking fertility drugs should be aware of the small potential risk of developing ovarian cancer. A risk that should be considered before taking fertility drugs. Two recent statistical studies have identified thirty-one cases of ovarian cancer developing in women who had taken fertility drugs.* Thankfully, the

---

*A. S. Whittemore, R. Harris, J. Itnyre, J. Halpern, and the Collaborative Ovarian Cancer Group, "Characteristics Relating to Ovarian Cancer Risk. Collaborative Analysis of Twelve U.S. Case Control Studies," *American Journal of Epidemiology* 136 (1992): 1184–1203, and M. A. Rossing, J. R. Daling, N. S. Weiss, D. E. Moore, and S. G. Self, "Ovarian Tumors in a Cohort of Infertile Women," *New England Journal of Medicine* 331 (1994): 771–76.

number of ovarian cancer cases is small, but these reports should not be ignored.*

What is the connection? One theory is the *incessant ovulation* theory. Think about it. The purpose of any fertility drug is to increase the rate of ovulation. A small percentage of women taking fertility drugs not only ovulate, they *superovulate.* One investigator estimates that a single stimulated cycle with fertility drugs may equal about two years of normal ovulation in a menstrual cycle.

The incessant ovulation theory holds that the more a woman ovulates without interruption or resting of the ovaries by pregnancy or oral contraceptives, the greater are her chances of developing ovarian cancer. This theory is based on solid data demonstrating that taking oral contraceptives can reduce a woman's risk of ovarian cancer by as much as 50 percent compared to those who have never taken oral contraceptives. And there is also a significant decrease in the ovarian cancer risk with increasing number of pregnancies, regardless of outcome, compared to those women who have never been pregnant.

Researchers speculate that every ovulation damages the surface of the ovaries. And, like any bodily injury, the body's normal repair mechanisms are called on to make the repair. However, the more the uninterrupted ovulations that occur, with the increased damage to the ovaries, the higher the probability that one of these damages will not be repaired and will eventually lead to abnormal cell division and ovarian cancer.

FAMILY HISTORY OF OVARIAN OR BREAST CANCER

Gilda Radner died on May 20, 1989, after a long, courageous battle against ovarian cancer. Regrettably, neither she nor her hus-

---

*See Appendix, Table 2.5: "Ovarian Cancer & Use of Fertility Drugs," and Appendix, Table 2.6: "Ovarian Cancer & Use of the Fertility Drug Clomid (Seattle, Washington, Study)."

band, Gene Wilder, ever knew at the time that Gilda's family history of ovarian and breast cancer put her at high risk for contracting the disease. Gilda knew only that her first cousin Lenore had ovarian cancer, but thought Lenore's mother had *stomach cancer.* Through the Familial Ovarian Cancer Registry, we now know that Gilda's aunt had ovarian cancer, not stomach cancer. We also know that another cousin had ovarian cancer and that possibly Gilda's maternal grandmother, who died of "*stomach cancer,*" could have had ovarian cancer. In addition, Gilda's mother had breast cancer. All of these factors put Gilda at an extremely high risk of developing the disease that eventually took her life.

It is commonly accepted that cancer results from a series of genetic (DNA) changes that disrupt normal cell growth. The process of cancer development also appears to have two steps: *initiation* and *promotion* (i.e., the initial alteration of cells exposed to a cancer-causing agent [e.g., tobacco smoke] so that they are likely to form a tumor with subsequent exposure to a promoting agent).

DNA is a well-known acronym for deoxyribonucleic acid, but what it stands for isn't as important as what it does. Simply, DNA stores all of our genetic information in pairs of four chemicals—adenine, cytosine, guanine, and thymine—and provides instructions which enable cells to grow normally. When the order of the four chemicals is incorrect, a mutation occurs which instructs cells to grow abnormally. This information can be passed on from one generation to the next. We believe that about 5 to 7 percent of ovarian cancer is inherited.

The BRCA1 gene is thought to cause ovarian cancer and breast cancer that runs in families. That is, in these families, the daughter of a mother with ovarian cancer may inherit an abnormal matched form of the BRCA1 gene. This mutation instructs cells to grow abnormally (the initiation step), and potentially results in ovarian cancer in the daughter. BRCA1 gene mutations are responsible in 80 percent of families with multiple cases of ovarian cancer. This mutation can be inherited from the mother or the father. Therefore, the daughter of a mother from a family with multiple close relatives with ovarian cancer has a 50-50 chance of inheriting the abnormal gene since she receives half of her genes from her mother and half from her father.

This abnormal gene by itself, however, does not result in ovarian cancer. If it did, daughters who inherited the BRCA1 mutation would have ovarian cancer at birth or at a very young age. There must be some other environmental factor (diet, talc, never pregnant, etc.) later in life that triggers the normal matched form of the BRCA1 gene to be nonfunctional (the promotion step). The presence of the mutant BRCA1 gene at birth and the subsequent loss of the normal matched form of the gene later in life stops normal cell growth, and causes abnormal cell growth known as ovarian cancer (see Table 2.1).

Until recently, there was little evidence in the medical literature on the genetic origin of some ovarian cancers. Our interest at Roswell was piqued in 1977, when we had a family in which five members spanning three generations (a grandmother, three daughters, and a granddaughter) had developed ovarian cancer. A year later, five members of a family spanning two generations (three sisters, a first cousin, and her daughter) came under our care for ovarian cancer. We reviewed the medical literature and found only five instances of familial (i.e., two or more first-degree relatives [mother, sister, daughter]) ovarian cancer identified between 1930 and 1970. But between 1970 and 1979, an additional twenty-six cases were reported. Because of the apparent increase in frequency in the decade of the 1970s, we established a registry in 1981 to further evaluate familial ovarian cancer in the United States. This Registry, renamed the Gilda Radner Familial Ovarian Cancer Registry in 1990, in memory of the late comedienne, has enrolled 1,297 families (with 3,281 cases of ovarian cancer) through 1995 (see Table 2.2). All families in the Registry have two or more first- or second-degree relatives (grandmother, aunts) with ovarian cancer and 40 percent have three or more first-degree relatives with the disease. In addition, there are over four hundred cases of breast cancer in the Reg-

Table 2.1

BRCAI Gene Mutations in 1% of Eastern European Jews
185 delAG Mutation

Normal Sequence
GCT ATG CAG AAA ATC TTA G̲AG ⟶ normal protein produced

Abnormal Sequence
GCT ATG CAG AAA ATC TTA G̲TG ⟶ non-functional protein produced

Each three letter genetic code sequence engineers the production of a single amino acid, the structural blocks that make a protein. In the 185delAG, the AG (Adenine and Guanine) are deleted from the normal sequence resulting in a non-functional protein.

When the amino acids are in this normal sequence, a normal protein is produced which acts to prevent an abnormal production of ovarian cells and subsequent ovarian cancer. When there is an amino acid substitution (here TG for AG), a nonfunctional or abnormal protein is produced which allows for the abnormal growth of the ovarian cancer cells and the development of ovarian cancer.

*   *   *

istry, including seventy-eight patients with both breast and ovarian cancer.

The definition of familial ovarian cancer syndrome has never been clearly established. While the debate and the confusion continue in the medical-scientific community, the general public also has difficulty in evaluating its risk for a possible familial history of ovarian cancer because of

- very small family size

- only male offspring

- early age of female deaths before ovarian cancer can develop

- rarely, unknown paternity

- difficulty in obtaining medical records that might document whether a close relative had ovarian cancer

Table 2.2

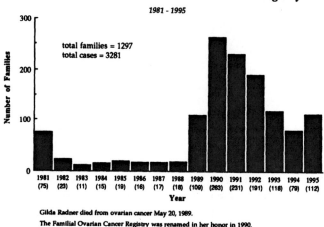

Gilda Radner Familial Ovarian Cancer Registry

1981 - 1995

total families = 1297
total cases = 3281

Gilda Radner died from ovarian cancer May 20, 1989.
The Familial Ovarian Cancer Registry was renamed in her honor in 1990.

- the possibility that ovarian cancers are misdiagnosed, and that on re-review the close family member did indeed have ovarian cancer.

The reality of both the confusion and the importance of the Registry in the public's perception is exemplified in this 1993 letter:

Thank you for your letter of kindness and information and for registering me with the Gilda Radner Familial Ovarian Cancer Registry (because of my own history of ovarian cancer). I'm so very pleased that there is such an organization for this type of cancer. I want to express some thoughts that I feel important to other women who may be in the same situation that I am in with my family history. My mother's family came from Czechoslovakia in the 1800s, they were a farming family, and records of births and deaths are rare from that time up until maybe fifty years ago. I just want to stress that I do not know if my family has a history of cancer. Most died on their farms and no autopsies were done at that time. Many believe that family members just died of whatever was going around at that time or of natural causes. I believe that there were some members who did die of certain cancers, but no one remaining in my mother's family knows. I hope you consider these facts and do not think of excluding women who have a family history such as mine.

It is often reported that a family history of breast cancer (mother, sister, daughter) increases one's risk for the development of ovarian cancer. The amount of increased risk ranges from none to 1.5 times (2.7 percent) that of the general population (whose risk is usually set at 1.8 percent). Gilda Radner's mother, Henrietta Radner, had battled with breast cancer but survived. Given the risk factors for ovarian cancer that have been discussed, it seems unlikely that Gilda Radner could have been spared this disease. However, given these facts, could the diagnosis of advanced ovarian cancer have been made earlier?

Table 2.3

Increased Risk of Ovarian Cancer

Risk Factors	Increased Risk
High-Fat Diet	0–2
High-Lactose Diet	
(Yogurt/Cottage Cheese	0–1.7
Never Pregnant	0–2
Infertility	0–1.8
Fertility-Stimulating Drugs	0–2
Talcum Powder	0–1.9
Estrogen Hormone Replacement	
Therapy (6–10 years)	0–1.4
Family History of Breast Cancer	0–1.5
Family History of Ovarian Cancer	4.5–18
No or Unknown Risk Factors	1 in 55 or 1.8% lifetime

Figure 2.3

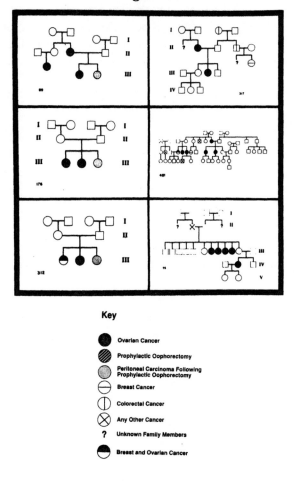

Key

⬤ Ovarian Cancer

◨ Prophylactic Oophorectomy

▦ Peritoneal Carcinoma Following Prophylactic Oophorectomy

⊖ Breast Cancer

⊕ Colorectal Cancer

⊗ Any Other Cancer

? Unknown Family Members

◓ Breast and Ovarian Cancer

M. S. Piver, "Prophylactic Oophorectomy and Ovarian Cancer Mortality," in *Cancer Prevention Series 1993*, edited by V. T. DeVita, Jr., S. Hellman, and S. A. Rosenberg (Philadelphia: J. B. Lippincott Company, 1992), pp. 1–10.

The pedigree of six families with a strong family history of ovarian cancer (solid circles) in which a family member developed a primary peritoneal carcinoma (dotted circles) similar in appearance to ovarian carcinoma after undergoing prophylactic removal of the ovaries (oophorectomy) to try to prevent the development of ovarian cancer.

Chapter 3

Prevention of Ovarian Cancer

Dear Mr. Wilder:

When Gilda's book came out in the spring of 1989, Ginny immediately purchased a copy and stayed up that night reading it. I cannot tell you how much comfort Ginny found in reading Gilda's words. Here, at last, was another woman, exactly her own age, fighting the same battle she had been fighting for eight years.

When Gilda wrote of her experiences with chemotherapy, radiation, and CT scans, Ginny knew—all too well—about these ordeals. When Gilda wrote about her feelings of fear, anger, despair and doubt, Ginny could empathize with her as only another cancer patient can. When Gilda visualized cancer cells as *stupid cells* that could be shot down by chemo, she gave Ginny the courage to take stronger treatments of chemo even if it meant the loss of her hair. If Gilda could accept this, then so could she. It helped Ginny to know that someone who loved life as much as she did was also fighting so hard to live. I only wish Ginny and Gilda could have met.

Ginny gave me Gilda's book to read. The first time I read it

I could only read a few pages at a time. When I saw how similar the experiences and feelings Gilda and Ginny shared, I would break down crying and further reading was impossible. Since then, I have read it many times. At Ginny's memorial service, I quoted Gilda when she wrote of cancer patients as "brave warriors battling cancer."

I have read of your outstanding efforts in the fight against ovarian cancer—how you have established the Gilda Radner Familial Ovarian Cancer Registry in Buffalo. How you appeared before a House subcommittee on May 9 and have done televised public service announcements warning women of symptoms of ovarian cancer. How proud Gilda would be of you and your work!

N. C.

INTRODUCTION

As you've read by now, several factors have been associated with the development of ovarian cancer. Some of these associations are stronger than others. Nevertheless, research has established that each factor could play at least a small role.

The question, then, is: If we know what can cause ovarian cancer, do we know what measures women can take to prevent it or at least to decrease their risk of developing the disease?

Fortunately, a number of measures have been identified that offer women some degree of protection against ovarian cancer. For example, women can decide to reduce the level of fat in their diet, and eliminate or limit their use of talcum powder. These decisions are easy to make and their merits are obvious. However, deciding the merits of other preventive measures— whether to use oral contraceptives, to become pregnant, to breast feed, to have tubal ligation for contraception, or to have normal ovaries removed during a hysterectomy for nonmalignant diseases or due to a family history of ovarian cancer (for the record, this procedure is called *prophylactic oophorectomy*)—may not be as easy.

Let's take a look at each of these.

ORAL CONTRACEPTIVES

Many recent studies have shown that using oral contraceptives (generically "the pill") protects women from ovarian cancer to some extent. However, results of a 1993 survey of female students and faculty employees at Yale University found that 80 percent of those responding weren't aware of this. In fact, in another survey, this time a Gallup poll, most female respondents believed that oral contraceptives caused significant complications, and cancer was at the top of the list.*

Here's what you should know.

In a 1987 study at the Centers for Disease Control (CDC), researchers compared 546 women with ovarian cancer to a control group of 4,228 women. They found that women who used oral contraceptives reduced their risk of ovarian cancer by 40 percent. They also found that the level of ovarian cancer risk continued to decrease the longer women used oral contraceptives, approaching 80 percent in women who used them for ten or more years. In a 1992 Collaborative Ovarian Cancer Group study, any use of oral contraceptives was associated with a decreased risk of ovarian cancer of 34 percent; but the decrease approached 70 percent for women using oral contraceptives for six years or more.

In another CDC study, researchers reported that women with

---

*See Appendix, Table 3.1: "Oral Contraceptive Use & Decreased Risk of Ovarian Cancer: Cancer and Steroid Hormone Study Group."

a family history of ovarian cancer (a mother, sister, daughter, grandmother, or aunt), but who had used oral contraceptives for ten years, reduced their risk of contracting ovarian cancer to a level below that of women with no family history of the disease and of women who had never used oral contraceptives. This is good news for women with a family history of ovarian cancer, because the protective, beneficial effects of using oral contraceptives appear to apply to them as well. These researchers concluded: "The demonstrated substantial noncontraceptive benefits from oral contraceptives justifies their judicious use as a potentially powerful resource for primary prevention in women at high risk of ovarian cancer."*

The protective effects of using oral contraceptives are consistent with the *incessant ovulation theory,* which proposes, as you'll recall, that uninterrupted ovulation causes repeated trauma to the ovary and eventually leads to ovarian cancer. Thus, because oral contraceptives inhibit ovulation, the repeated monthly trauma to the ovary is decreased significantly.

PREGNANCY

Pregnancy protects against the development of ovarian cancer in a similar fashion as the use of oral contraceptives. This may, at least partially, explain the low incidence of ovarian cancer in Third World countries, where the tradition of very large families continues. Results of a 1992 study by the Collaborative Ovarian Cancer Group demonstrated that ovarian cancer risk was reduced by 40 percent in women with one pregnancy, and further decreased by

---

*T. P. Gross and J. J. Schlesselman, "The Estimated Effect of Oral Contraceptive Use on the Cumulative Risk of Epithelial Ovarian Cancer," *Obstetrics and Gynecology* 83 (1994): 419–24.

14 percent for each subsequent pregnancy. For women with six or more pregnancies, risk was reduced by 71 percent.*

A 1994 case-control study from Southern Ontario, Canada, also supports the protective effect of pregnancy. Researchers demonstrated that for each additional pregnancy, there was increasing protection against ovarian cancer. The highest protection was reported in women who had four or more pregnancies, but even one or more reduced the risk of ovarian cancer by 61 percent.

BREAST FEEDING

Breast feeding is believed to reduce the risk of ovarian cancer by either suppressing incessant ovulation or suppressing pituitary hormone production. Some researchers have assumed that because ovulation often resumes before a woman stops breast feeding, especially women who breast feed for a prolonged period of time, only about half of the protective effect of breast feeding is due to suppression of ovulation. Regardless of which mechanism provides what percentage of the effect, research evidence appears to support the role of breast feeding in protecting women from ovarian cancer.†

Between 1980 and 1982, for example, the Cancer and Steroid Hormone Study Group evaluated the detailed history of breast feeding in women ages forty to fifty-five, who were recently diagnosed with ovarian cancer. They discovered that women who breast fed for only one to two months decreased their risk of ovarian cancer by about 40 percent, compared to women who had never breast fed. Unlike more pregnancies or prolonged use

---

*See Appendix, Table 3.2: "Pregnancy & Decreased Risk of Ovarian Cancer: Collaborative Ovarian Cancer Group Study."

†See Appendix, Table 3.3: "Breast Feeding & Decreased Risk of Ovarian Cancer: Cancer and Hormone Study Group."

of oral contraceptives, however, there was no significant further reduction of risk related to duration of breast feeding. The only exception was women who breast fed for two or more years, who had a decreased risk approaching 70 percent.

This study also found that women who had been pregnant, who had breast fed, or who had used oral contraceptives reduced their risk of ovarian cancer by 40, 45, and 50 percent respectively, compared to women who had not experienced any of these exposures, even when each factor was considered separately. The mechanism of protection is consistent with the fact that all three inhibit ovulation.

In a 1993 multinational study that included Australia, Chile, Israel, Mexico, the Philippines, and Thailand—countries where women breast feed for prolonged periods of time—researchers observed a 20 to 25 percent decrease in risk among women who breast feed from three to seven months. However, there was little further reduction in risk with increasing months of breast feeding. The authors concluded that the short-term breast feeding practices common in developed countries may provide as great a reduction in the risk of ovarian cancer as the long-term breast feeding practice common in the developing countries studied.

TUBAL LIGATION

Tubal ligation is a surgical form of female sterilization which is referred to colloquially as *having your tubes tied*. During the procedure, the fallopian tubes are closed off or tied by a variety of mechanical methods. Tubal ligation has only recently been shown to decrease the risk of ovarian cancer, as a result of the Nurses Health Study of 121,700 married, female registered nurses, ages thirty to fifty-five, between 1976 and 1988.*

*See Appendix, Table 3.4: "Tubal Ligation & Decreased Risk of Ovarian Cancer: The Nurses Health Study: 1976–1988."

In a detailed questionnaire, participants were asked if they used any form of contraception and, if so, to specify if they used oral contraceptives, rhythm, diaphragm, condom, intrauterine device, foam or jelly, tubal ligation, or husband's vasectomy. Women who reported having had cancer, who had had one or both ovaries removed, or who were postmenopausal were excluded, leaving 77,544 women for evaluation. During the study period, 157 cases of ovarian cancer were confirmed in premenopausal women. Fourteen percent of these women had reported having tubal ligation. When compared to women in the study who had not had tubal ligation, there was a 71 percent reduction in the risk of developing ovarian cancer.

There are many theories to explain the decreased risk afforded by this procedure. One holds that tubal ligation inhibits the transport of talc to the ovary. However, these researchers reported that tubal ligation was also highly protective in women who reported never using talc.

Others who analyzed the study suggest that tubal ligation prevents the upward flow from the vagina of other toxins yet to be implicated in causing ovarian cancer. These could include, for example, contraceptive foams or gels. However, to date, there is no evidence that either harms the ovaries. Still others propose that tubal ligation decreases the blood supply to the ovaries and, therefore, lowers the hormone levels that could reach and influence the ovarian cells to become malignant.

Whichever theory (if any or all) holds the final answer, the researchers suggest tubal ligation has a demonstrated protective effect against ovarian cancer which should be considered as an option when women are deciding on a method of contraception.

REMOVAL OF OVARIES DURING HYSTERECTOMY FOR NONMALIGNANT DISEASE

The question facing many women age forty and older, who are about to undergo a hysterectomy for noncancerous uterine conditions such as uterine fibroids, is whether having their ovaries removed during the procedure will lower their odds of developing ovarian cancer. The question is very important. The individual decision is very personal and each woman must weigh the psychological effects of removing her ovaries against the psychological effects of the threat of developing ovarian cancer.

A major medical argument against removing the ovaries is that the ovaries function normally at age forty prior to menopause. However, it is well documented that: (1) many women have menopausal symptoms (hot flashes) while still menstruating, indicating a significant loss of function of the ovaries; (2) some women develop osteoporosis by age forty; (3) fertility decreases significantly after age forty; and (4) estrogen levels decrease at age forty. Each is consistent with a significant decrease in ovarian function after age forty and before menopause.

Hormone replacement (estrogen) therapy is another medical argument against the procedure. One concern is that compliance with hormone replacement therapy is low, even though it is well known that such therapy helps prevent symptoms of menopause, is very protective against heart disease, and prevents osteoporosis. A second concern is that hormone replacement therapy increases a woman's lifetime risk of breast cancer.

This latter concern was elevated to a controversy in June 1995, following a report in the *New England Journal of Medicine* which concluded that hormone replacement therapy, with or without progesterones,* increased the breast cancer risk in post-

---

*Progesterone: one of the two female hormones, the other being estrogen.

menopausal women. In human terms, this meant that rather than the seven cases of breast cancer expected to occur over a ten-year period in 200 women age fifty-five, a total ten cases would be expected to develop if all women in this age group used hormones. To put the risk in perspective, if the study is correct, a sixty-year-old woman who had used hormone replacement therapy for at least five years had a 3 percent chance of developing breast cancer over the next five years, compared to 1.8 percent chance of developing breast cancer for a woman who had never used hormone therapy after menopause.

But wait! Only a few weeks later (here we go again!), on July 12, 1995, an article in the *Journal of the American Medical Association* concluded that hormone replacement therapy was not associated with an increased risk of breast cancer. And, believe it or not, the results indicated that long-term use (eight or more years) of estrogen and progesterone hormone replacement therapy may have actually reduced the risk of breast cancer, and further that there was no association between very long-term (twenty or more years) use and breast cancer.

These conflicting data tell us one thing: If women taking hormone replacement therapy are at any increased risk at all of contracting breast cancer, it must be very small.

Still the questions remain: Should normal ovaries be removed in women age forty or over? And if so, how many cases of ovarian cancer might be prevented each year? Each year in the United States, 600,000 women have hysterectomies. Each woman age forty and older has the opportunity to eliminate the risk of ovarian cancer by having her ovaries removed during the procedure. However, a 1993 report by the CDC indicates that this is not the choice being made. Of the 1,711,257 women having hysterectomies in the United States between 1988 and 1990, about 40 percent of those age forty and older who underwent the procedure for a benign uterine condition chose not to have their ovaries removed. And a 1993 study by the American College of Surgeons gives us at least some clue as to a specific number of cases of ovarian cancer that might be prevented each year. Researchers reviewed 12,316 cases of women with ovarian cancer and found that 10 percent had had a hysterectomy at age forty or older, and that they could have potentially been spared their disease if their ovaries had been removed at that time.

REMOVAL OF OVARIES FOR A FAMILY HISTORY OF OVARIAN CANCER

In one of the most frequently cited reports on the risk of ovarian cancer in families with one first-degree relative (a mother, sister, or daughter) with the disease, in 1988 researchers from the Cancer and Steroid Hormone Study Group evaluated 493 women with ovarian cancer and compared them to a control group of 2,465 women. The results showed that for any first-degree relative, the lifetime risk of ovarian cancer increased to 6.5 percent. (Remember, the lifetime risk for women without a family history of cancer is 1.8 percent.) However, if the first-degree relative was the mother, the lifetime risk in the daughters increased to 7.5 percent. Although not as high as the 10 percent risk by age eighty for breast cancer, this is still a significant risk for a disease that has no highly accurate screening methods.

Daughters of women who had ovarian cancer also have to be concerned about the age at which their mothers were diagnosed. Researchers from the Ovarian Screening Clinic at Kings College Hospital, in the United Kingdom, who in 1993 studied 391 ovarian cancer families, reported that the younger the mother was when diagnosed with ovarian cancer, the greater the daughter's risk of contracting the disease. They found that when the mother was diagnosed before age forty-five, the daughter's lifetime risk increased to 25 percent; when diagnosed between ages forty-five and fifty-four, the lifetime risk increased to 9 percent; and when diagnosed after age fifty-five, the lifetime risk increased to about 6 percent. Overall, the increased lifetime risk was 8 percent, almost the same as that reported by the Cancer and Steroid Hormone Study Group.

The evaluation of families enrolled in the Gilda Radner Familial Ovarian Cancer Registry is consistent with an autosomal dominant pattern of inheritance. What? You're right, sorry! *Autosomal* refers to the origin of the mutated gene being a chromosome other than a sex chromosome. *Dominant* means that the entire mutated gene is transmitted, unchanged, to the offspring. Remember what they tried to teach us in biology about the Austrian geneticist Gregor Mendel and his experiments with peas? In 1865, Mendel described his study with peas: "Those characteristics that are transmitted entire, or almost unchanged by hybridization . . . are termed *dominant,* and those that become latent in the process are termed recessive."

But what does it really mean? This autosomal dominant pattern of inheritance suggests a 50 percent probability of inheriting the gene in first-degree relatives (a mother, sister, or daughter), 25 percent in second-degree relatives (a grandmother or aunt), and 12.5 percent in third-degree relatives (cousins). Because of these high risks, the Registry, from 1984 until now, has recommended that women with two or more first-degree relatives or first-and second-degree relatives with ovarian cancer should consider having their ovaries removed after age thirty-five, if they have completed their families. Now, however, unless or until the information on increased risk reported is confirmed by other centers, the Registry recommends that women with only one first-degree relative with ovarian cancer not have their ovaries removed.

Video laparoscopy is the surgical procedure recommended for removal of the ovaries (without hysterectomy), due to its low morbidity and the minimal disruption caused in the lives of these women. At the time of the procedure, the pelvis and abdomen should be examined carefully. Both ovaries should be submitted for pathologic evaluation to ensure that no very small ovarian cancer is missed by the naked eye. Patients then receive hormone re-placement therapy (estrogen and progesterone), and have a phys-ical examination and CA125 test annually or every six months.

Of concern in recommending the removal of the ovaries were reports of a small number of these women developing pap-illary carcinoma* of the peritoneum.† Because of this concern, the Registry surveyed the first 931 families (2,221 total cases) enrolled between 1981 and 1992. Of the 324 women who had had their ovaries removed for reasons of familial ovarian cancer, six (1.8 percent) developed papillary carcinoma of the peri-toneum from one to twenty-seven years after their surgery. Although this is very uncommon, women who are having their ovaries removed should be told of the small risk.

As you read earlier, we believe that between 5 and 7 percent of ovarian cancer is familial in nature. Therefore, removal of the ovaries in women with a family history of ovarian cancer could result in the prevention of between 1,330 (5 percent) and 1,860 (7 percent) of the estimated 26,600 cases diagnosed each year.

The quick reference list below sums up the significant decreases in the risk of ovarian cancer when the practices, behav-iors, choices, and procedures indicated are elected by women.

---

*For papillary carcinoma, see chapter 5.

†The peritoneum is a thin layer that lines the abdominal cavity and covers most of the abdominal organs, including the ovaries.

Protection against Ovarian Cancer

Factors	Decreased Ovarian Cancer Risk
Oral Contraceptives	40 percent
Pregnancy	40 percent
Breast Feeding	40 percent
Tubal Ligation	71 percent
Removal of Ovaries in Women age 40 or over at Hysterectomy for Noncancerous Condition of Uterus	10 percent*
Removal of Ovaries for a Family History of Ovarian Cancer	5–7 percent*

*Decrease in the total number of cases of ovarian cancer in the U.S. per year

Chapter 4

Diagnosing Ovarian Cancer

Dear Mr. Wilder:

On Tuesday, May 8, 1990, I saw you speak about your wife Gilda and her fight with ovarian cancer on Connie Chung's CBS television show. As you described Gilda's symptoms, I felt a chill wash through my body and I knew that I too had ovarian cancer.

On Tuesday, May 22, just two weeks after your appearance, I underwent a total hysterectomy. I do indeed have ovarian cancer; however, my tumors are grade 1 and did not appear to have spread. I am now undergoing chemotherapy which will last until December.

I would like to add that we also share your sorrow in Gilda's loss. We loved her work always. We have long been fans of you and Gilda and your marriage seemed a perfect match.

                                                        C. F. F.

SYMPTOMS ASSOCIATED WITH OVARIAN CANCER

Ovarian cancer is often referred to as the *silent killer* because most people believe that by the time a woman has symptoms, the disease has already spread throughout her abdomen and beyond (that is, at stages III and IV). While it's true that the five-year survival rate for these patients is poor (less than 20 percent), it's also true that if ovarian cancer is diagnosed when still confined to the ovary (stage I), the five-year survival rate is 90 percent or better.

What isn't true is that the early stages of ovarian cancer (stages I and II) are universally *silent.* Symptoms most often associated with ovarian cancer include: a feeling of being bloated; clothes that don't fit quite as easily as they once did; vague abdominal and pelvic discomfort; and gastrointestinal symptoms such as gas, back pain, and fatigue.

Before you think it, I realize that many women have these vague symptoms from time to time, and they certainly should not fear they have ovarian cancer. However, these symptoms have occurred in a regular pattern often enough to be grouped as symptoms *associated* with ovarian cancer. Therefore, if any of these symptoms persists for more than several weeks, this may be an early warning of ovarian cancer and should not be ignored.

Results of a study that compared the *presenting symptoms* (those which first caused a woman to visit her doctor) in women with early-stage ovarian cancer and those with advanced disease indicated that abdominal swelling, abdominal pain, intestinal symptoms, vaginal bleeding, fatigue, and/or fever were common in both groups. Ninety percent of the women with early-stage disease reported some type of presenting symptom. So, as you can see, ovarian cancer is not so silent!*

Regrettably, Gilda Radner had almost all of the symptoms

---

*See Appendix, Table 4.1: "Symptoms of Early Localized and Nonlocalized Advanced Ovarian Cancer."

associated with the disease beginning in October 1985, and was finally diagnosed with advanced ovarian cancer in October 1986.

GILDA RADNER'S SYMPTOMS, 1985–1986[*]

Fatigue and Fever

(October 1985) "The last couple of weeks in England I just didn't have any energy. I slipped on the stairs in our flat and hit the small of my back. That slowed me down for weeks. I'd feel good for a few days and I'd think I was fine, and then I would wake up one day and feel like I was getting the flu. I'd think I had a fever, so from my life's experience with illness, I would say, 'I'm getting the flu.' "

(January 1986) "Then on a Sunday, maybe the first Sunday of 1986, Gene and I were in the car on our way to play tennis at a friend's house. Suddenly my eyelids got very heavy. It was as though I was hypnotized into this deep sleep. I had slept well the night before and I wasn't sick, but a feeling of uncomfortable tiredness came over me . . . like a fog rolling in over my brain that I couldn't escape. I was listless the rest of the day and slept that night and into the next day in that same relentless fog. It was a new element added to my on-and-off flu symptoms. It scared me. . . .

"In the next couple of weeks, I ran a low-grade fever. I called up the internist and said, 'I am running a fever.'

"He asked, 'How high?'

" 'Not much—very low—ninety-nine, a hundred.'

---

[*] *It's Always Something,* pp. 46–47, 48, 49, 51, 53, 58, 59, 70, 72.

"He said, 'It's nothing to worry about. Take aspirin or Tylenol to treat the fever—it can happen in this Epstein-Barr Virus.' "

Pelvic Pain

(April 1986) "During that month of April, I started having weird pelvic cramping. I went to see a gynecologist in Connecticut. He ran a series of blood tests that showed absolutely nothing wrong and he said what I had was mittelschmerz, meaning that during the time of ovulation I could sometimes get severe cramping."

Abdominal Pain and Bloating

(June 1986) "We spent one evening in Paris before flying back to America. I remember it was very hot, record temperatures for that time of year. The city felt close and steamy and even Sparkle couldn't stop panting in the heat. We ate our dinner at a favorite bistro on the Right Bank near the Louvre. After dinner I got a severe attack of stomach cramps. I'd eaten hardly anything because it was so humid, there wasn't any air conditioning in the restaurant. My stomach felt bloated and hard. When Gene and I left the bistro, I could barely walk in the streets. . . .

"But throughout the summer the pains in my stomach and bowels continued. I went to see my New York gynecologist. She did an exam and said that it was definitely a stomach problem. She suggested I see a gastroenterologist. I did, and he agreed that I had a stomach problem. I told him about the vitamins I was taking and he felt the high dosages of vitamin C could be causing the gas. He had me go off all the vitamins that I was taking. He was skeptical of the Epstein-Barr Virus diagnosis. He thought my problems were emotional. He had heard that my recent movie hadn't done well. It was the return of the Queen of Neurosis. He felt that most stomach problems are a result of stress and anxiety and can be controlled by getting the stress out of your life."

Leg Pain

(July 1986) "Then a new symptom appeared—an aching, gnawing pain in the upper thighs and in my legs. It started slowly, then increased and would not go away."

(October 1986) "On Tuesday, October 21, I drove to see the holistic doctor. He put me on a special powdered protein diet. I canceled my acupuncture appointment. The next day, I canceled my appointment for another colonic. I was in too much pain even to leave the house. On Thursday, October 23, Gene's secretary drove me to see the internist. My stomach was inflated like a balloon and I was too weak to drive myself. The internist did a pelvic exam. He checked me into the hospital immediately for tests."

Bowel Disturbance and Gas

(August 1986) "The gastroenterologist decided I should have a pelvic sonogram to rule out the possibility that any tumor or growth was pressing on a nerve and making my legs ache or causing the bowel disturbance and the gas."

(October 1986) "He [the gastroenterologist] checked me into the hospital merely for tests."

Abdominal Distention

(October 1986) "Friday morning, fluid was extracted from my swollen belly. . . .

"In the late afternoon or early evening on Friday, the internist came into the room. I was lying in the bed and Gene was sitting on the left side of my bed. We had been talking, absently watching television, while waiting for the reports to come in. We both looked up into the doctor's eyes as he said, very calmly, 'We've discovered there is a malignancy.' "

Not only did Gilda Radner have essentially every risk factor known for ovarian cancer—a family history of ovarian cancer, a family history of breast cancer, use of fertility-stimulating drugs, no full-term pregnancy, infertility, and a high-fat diet—but, sadly, she also had essentially every symptom associated with ovarian cancer.

Symptoms Associated with Ovarian Cancer

Associated Symptoms in the General Population	Dates of Gilda Radner's Associated Symptoms
Fever	October 1985
Feeling Tired	October 1985
Pelvic Pain	April 1986
Bloated Feeling	June 1986
Abdominal Discomfort	June 1986
Feeling of Intestinal Gas	August 1986
Backache	October 1986

DIAGNOSTIC TESTS

In a perfect world, doctors would be able to order a single non-invasive (that is, nonsurgical) test that would determine for them and their patients if a suspicious pelvic mass discovered on physical examination was ovarian cancer. In the real world, however, and despite great advances in technology and current research, there is no such test available. Instead, doctors rely on the results of a series of tests which we will present here, and also on the willingness of their patients to endure them, as they work through the process of diagnosing ovarian cancer.

As you read about these diagnostic tests, remember that it is more important to be familiar with their names and have confidence in their value than it is to understand the science behind each test.

CA125 Blood Test

The CA125 blood test has been available since 1983, when researchers at Harvard University discovered that levels of this protein were elevated in 80 percent of women with one type of ovarian cancer (epithelial). CA125 levels have been shown to be elevated in 95 percent of women with advanced-stage (III and IV) ovarian cancer; but, unfortunately, only in 40 to 50 percent of women with stage I disease. CA125 levels also have been found to be elevated in a number of benign conditions, as well as in the first trimester of pregnancy.*

Because of this association with benign conditions, CA125 has been eliminated as a screening tool for ovarian cancer in the

---

*See Appendix, Table 4.2: "CA125 Levels Higher Than 35U/ml in Cancer."

Noncancerous Causes of Elevated CA125

Endometriosis	Ectopic occurrence of endometrial lining tissue frequently involving the ovaries
Pelvic Inflammatory Disease	Bacterial infection of the tubes and ovaries
Uterine Fibroids	Noncancerous tumors of the uterus
Uterine Adenomyosis	Ectopic endometrial lining tissue in the wall of the uterus
Ectopic Pregnancy	Pregnancy in the fallopian tube
Benign Ovarian Tumors	Nonmalignant ovarian tumors
Liver Disease	Liver Disease
Pancreatitis	Inflammation of the pancreas
Peritonitis	Inflammation of the abdominal or perioneal cavity
Renal Failure	Kidney Failure
Heart Failure	Heart Failure
First Trimester Pregnancy	Pregnancy within the first three months
Menstruation	Menstruation

Figure 4.1

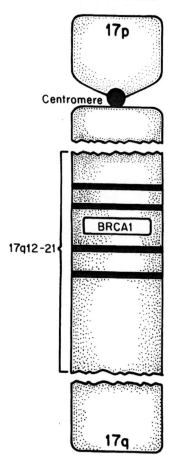

Location of the BRCAI gene on the long arm (q) of chromosome 17. The BRCAI gene is responsible for most inherited ovarian or breast cancers.

general population. But, for women who have symptoms associated with ovarian cancer and who understand that it is elevated in only 50 percent of early cancers, CA125 is an excellent test.

Ultrasound

"The gastroenterologist decided that I should have a pelvic sonogram to rule out the possibility that any tumor or growth was pressing on a nerve and making my legs ache or causing the bowel disturbance and the gas. The sonogram showed there was some congestion. My ovaries weren't exactly in the place where they were supposed to be, but that wasn't serious. There was no sign of tumor, no sign of obstruction or a mass, and they sent me home saying, 'Everything is fine—there is nothing to worry about.' " (*It's Always Something*, pp. 59–60)

Ultrasound should be prescribed for women with symptoms associated with ovarian cancer and those with a suspicious mass in the pelvis. Simply stated, ultrasound is the most effective, safest noninvasive method doctors have of *seeing* into the pelvis to determine and evaluate the physical characteristics of the ovaries—their size, shape and configuration, consistency and whether they are cystic, solid, or both (see Figure 4.2).

Ultrasound is based on the principle that solid masses, such as tumors, reflect sound waves. By placing an ultrasound probe on the abdominal wall over the ovaries (*transabdominal*) or in the vagina near the ovaries (*transvaginal*), reflected sound waves can be collected and transmitted onto a screen, creating a snapshot of the pelvis for evaluation. Obviously, the better the snapshot, the better the evaluation. For that reason, transvaginal ultrasound is preferred by most doctors because the probe can be placed closer to the ovaries, resulting in improved image quality of better resolution (see Figures 4.3 and 4.4).

Figure 4.2

**Ultrasonographic Patterns of Ovarian Cysts
and Malignant Tumors**

Benign Ovarian Cysts

   ◯ Simple cyst without internal echoes

   ◌ Simple cyst with scattered pinpoint echoes

   ⊗ Cyst with thin septums

Malignant Ovarian Cysts

   ◉ Cystic echoes with papillary structures

   ⊛ Cystic echoes with irregular thick septum and solid parts

   ● Partly solid pattern with irregular cystic part

   ● Completely solid

Transvaginal Color Flow Doppler

While ultrasound *snapshots* provide doctors with excellent documentation of the physical characteristics and the condition of the ovaries, they do not provide enough specific information to enable the doctor to reliably determine which abnormal conditions are cancerous and which are not. A test called *transvaginal color flow doppler* is a step forward in helping make this distinction, and should be the next diagnostic test ordered if the results of the ultrasound are suspicious.

First, a little biology: Cancerous ovarian tumors need new blood vessels to supply the nourishment they need to grow;

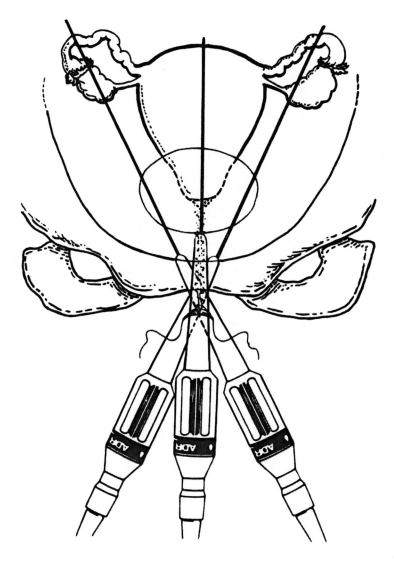

Diagrammatic illustration of a transvaginal ultrasound probe in the vagina. With the probe in the vagina in closer proximity to the ovaries, the ultrasound view of the ovaries is improved.

Figure 4.4

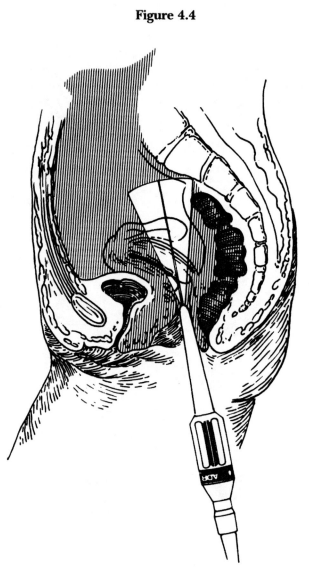

Cross-sectional view of the transvaginal ultrasound probe in the vagina and its close proximity to the ovaries. This gives improved images of the ovaries because of the closeness of the probe to the ovaries in contrast to abdominal ultrasound which has to transmit more distant signals.

benign ovarian cysts are nourished by normal blood vessels. These newly formed tumor blood vessels are smaller and weaker than normal blood vessels. Also, they offer much less (in fact, very little) resistance as blood flows through them than do normal blood vessels.

Transvaginal color flow doppler technology* can pinpoint the characteristics of the blood vessels supplying the pelvic mass by using a vaginal probe to measure the speed and amount of resistance as the blood flows through the vessels. These measurements are recorded and displayed in the form of graphs that reflect the speed (*pulsatile index*) and the amount of resistance (*resistant index*). These indexes can be thought of as being similar to the diastolic and systolic readings when you have your blood pressure taken. Generally, lower values of either index indicate little resistance to blood flow and suggest new blood vessels and a cancerous tumor. Higher values of either index indicate greater resistance and suggest normal blood vessels and a benign ovarian cyst.

Transvaginal color flow doppler results aren't perfect, but their accuracy in determining if pelvic masses are cancerous ovarian tumors or benign ovarian cysts is high enough to be helpful in deciding if surgery might be needed.

CT Scan and MRI

"They took me downstairs to the radiation department and began running numerous tests on me. Blood was drawn. I had an ultrasound—to make sure I wasn't pregnant. I wasn't. Then came the CAT scan. The internist was there overseeing everything. I never had a CAT scan or anything like it in my life. The closest I ever came was when

---

*See Appendix, Table 4.4: "Transvaginal Color Flow Doppler in Differentiating Benign from Malignant Ovarian Tumors."

I saw the Woody Allen movie *Hannah and Her Sisters.* That movie did so much for me because I saw it right in the middle of all my weird illness and it confirmed the results of neurosis for me. I thought about how Woody Allen created his brain tumor. Good old Woody, he hit right on what's happening in my life, too, that this whole thing could be me just being neurotic. Except this wasn't a movie. It was really happening. It was my body going through the round eye of the CAT-scan machine. I became like a child. I put myself in other people's hands. . . .

"I think the internist went on to say that the malignancy was confirmed by the CAT scan and the analysis of the fluid from my belly. Surgery would have to be done as soon as possible. When he left the room, I grabbed Gene's face in my hands and sobbed." (*It's Always Something,* pp. 71–72)

CA125, transvaginal ultrasound, and color flow doppler are the primary noninvasive methods for diagnosing ovarian cancer. However, if the results of these tests are normal, yet symptoms persist, a computed axial tomography (CT) scan may be helpful in diagnosing ovarian cancer.

As the woman lies underneath the CT scanner, X-rays are taken of multiple cross-sections of the internal organs of the pelvis and abdomen which are assembled into three-dimensional images for viewing by the radiologist.

CT scans are used mainly to diagnose cancer that has spread to the lymph nodes, other abdominal organs, abdominal fluids (*ascites*), and the liver; and to measure the response to chemotherapy in women with ovarian cancer (see Figures 4.5 and 4.6).

Magnetic resonance imaging (MRI) uses nuclear magnetic resonance technology to create cross-sectional images of the pelvis and abdominal organs which are assembled into three-dimensional images for viewing by a radiologist. MRI has yet to add value to any of the other diagnostic tests for ovarian cancer.

Figure 4.5

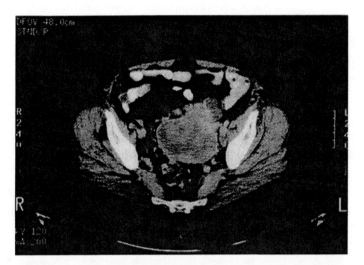

CT scan of the pelvis showing a very large ovarian cancer (large gray area in the center).

Figure 4.6

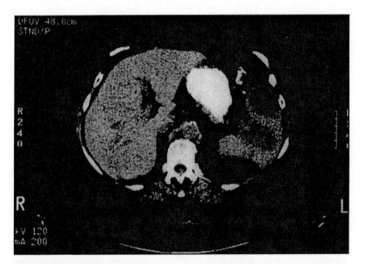

CT scan of the upper abdomen demonstrating a normal liver but a spleen with a large metastasis from the ovarian cancer (black area).

Outpatient Laparoscopy

Even with these great advances in technology, on rare occasions, outpatient laparoscopy may be required to determine if a malignant condition is present or not. In laparoscopy, the abdomen is first inflated with carbon dioxide and the laparoscope (which is a type of endoscope, i.e., an instrument for the examination of the interior of a hollow viscus), is passed through a small incision in the abdominal wall. Laparoscopy is frequently used to view the female reproductive organs and is now commonly used for removing gall bladders and ovaries when indicated. Unlike ultrasonography, CT scan, or MRI, laparoscopy allows for direct visualization of the pelvic and abdominal organs.

Chapter 5

The Thirty Different Types of Ovarian Cancer: The Pathology of Ovarian Cancer

Dear Mr. Wilder:

I have wanted to write to you for quite some time. I felt a need to express to you my sorrow for Gilda.

I, too, am a victim of ovarian cancer. It was diagnosed about one week apart from Gilda's. I am very happy to write that I was one of the extremely fortunate ladies who survived!

I read Gilda's book, *It's Always Something.* I loved it as I did her. I especially loved her doing Roseanne Roseannadanna! It is funny because when I was younger I used to watch Roseanne and marvel at this woman whom I thought to be so funny.

The book *It's Always Something* was hard for me to read and many sections sent chills through my spine because I could totally relate to this lady (who I admired so) and was going through all of this.

There were so many similarities in the book between my life and Gilda's. Our birthdays were one week apart and there were things about our families that were similar. If I remember correctly, we even lost our fathers around the same age, age fourteen?

We were diagnosed with ovarian cancer one week apart and went through all the therapy and surgeries almost identically. She was so right when she said in the book "there is nothing funny about cancer."

In the book I also remember reading how much support and love Gilda got from you when she was undergoing her treatments. That was some of the best medicine of all! I really admired that because my husband could not accept the fact that I was sick and reacted very poorly. It was a very hard time for all of us as I am sure you know.

C. H.

Dr. Robert E. Scully, a leading pathologist, once wrote the following in a text for physicians:

Knowledge of the pathology of ovarian tumors is essential to understanding their behavior and selecting the optimal therapy. The ovary is the site of a wider variety of tumors than any other organ, and the oft-repeated precept that ovarian neoplasia is not one but many diseases is fully justified by the range of its biological manifestations.*

There are three predominant classes of ovarian tumors: *common epithelial tumors, germ cell tumors,* and *sex cord-stromal tumors.* Common epithelial tumors, which will be described briefly here, account for 90 percent of all ovarian cancers, while germ cell and sex cord-stromal tumors, which won't be described here, account for only about 5 percent each. There are at least thirty different types of ovarian cancer within these three classes. Gilda Radner had a type of common epithelial cancer known as carcinoma, adenocarcinoma, or cystadenocarcinoma, all of which are in a sense the same cancer.

There are subtle and not so subtle microscopic differences between each classification and each type of ovarian cancer. The

---

*In M. S. Piver, ed., *Ovarian Malignancies: Diagnostic and Therapeutic Advances* (London: Churchill Livingston, 1987), p. 27.

ability of the pathologist to identify these differences is critically important to your physician in developing your treatment plan.

Knowing this is important to you because it highlights the complex nature of the ovary and ovarian cancer, and stresses the importance of early detection, accurate diagnosis and prompt, appropriate treatment.

COMMON EPITHELIAL OVARIAN CANCERS

What's in a Name?

Common epithelial ovarian cancers originate in the cells of the tissue (epithelium) that either covers or lines the ovary. Cancers that originate in epithelial cells are called *carcinomas*. Cancers that arise from *glandular* epithelial cells in the ovary are called *adenocarcinomas*, and those that have a *cystic* component are called *cystadenocarcinomas*. Another type, *borderline ovarian carcinomas* (*carcinomas of low malignant potential*), will be described later.

Common epithelial ovarian cancers fall into five major subtypes, based on their cell type and origin: *serous* (50 percent), *endometrioid* (15 percent), *mucinous* (10 percent), *clear cell* (5 percent), and *Brenner's* (1 percent). About 1 percent of all women will develop the most common epithelial ovarian cancer, namely, *serous adenocarcinoma.**

The remaining common epithelial ovarian cancers—about 20 percent—are referred to as *undifferentiated* because their exact cell of origin cannot be determined microscopically. And, to complicate matters further, there are mixed common epithelial cancers that contain a significant component of a second or third subtype.

---

*See Appendix, Table 5.1: "Common Epithelial Ovarian Cancers."

We don't know yet why this is the case, but clear cell carcinomas, even when still confined to the ovary, are the toughest to deal with in terms of response to therapy and long-term survival. At this point, chemotherapy, because it destroys cancer cells, appears to be the treatment that offers the most hope for improving long-term outcome.

On rare occasions, an ovarian cancer will contain both *carcinoma* elements and those of a cell type known as *sarcoma*. Sarcomas arise from the connective tissue inside the ovary, whereas carcinomas arise from the epithelium that covers or lines the ovary. Of importance to patients who have *mixed ovarian carcinoma* or *sarcoma* is that these cancers are treated with different types of chemotherapy than ovarian carcinoma, and that survival is significantly worse.

Grade of Tumor

Knowing the type of ovarian cancer (e.g., clear cell) is only the first step in understanding the behavior of a particular ovarian cancer and selecting the appropriate treatment. Each of these cell types is *graded* based on the aggressive, i.e., abnormal, microscopic appearance of the cells that make up the cancer. Pathologists are trained to evaluate the degree of microscopic aggressiveness, which is referred to as grade or differentiation. Women with grade 1 (well-differentiated) or grade 2 (moderately differentiated) ovarian carcinomas have a significantly better chance for long-term survival than women with grade 3 (poorly differentiated) ovarian carcinomas (see chapters 6 and 7; see also Figure 5.1).

Borderline Ovarian Tumors

Borderline ovarian carcinomas or *carcinomas of low malignant potential* are interesting because they don't behave as completely benign or as frankly malignant.* Borderline ovarian carcinomas occur ten to fifteen years earlier than frankly malignant ovarian cancers. Most importantly, they have a significantly better prognosis. When confined to the ovary, borderline ovarian carcinomas have a long-term survival approaching 100 percent, compared to 85 to 90 percent in frankly malignant ovarian cancers. Even when borderline ovarian carcinomas spread outside the ovary (metastasize)—a common first sign of being frankly malignant—the long-term survival is 80 to 92 percent at five years, compared to 15 to 20 percent for those that are frankly malignant.

Finally!

How much the physician discloses about the cell type that makes up the tumor, its grade, or if it is borderline in nature depends on how much detail the patient and her family want or need. There is no question, however, that ovarian cancer is complex—with thirty different types in all—and that all women should know the importance of early detection, accurate diagnosis and prompt, appropriate treatment.

---

*Benign carcinomas are unable to spread or metastasize and cause death, whereas frankly malignant carcinomas are able to spread or metastasize and cause death.

Figure 5.1

Histologic Grading of Ovarian Cancers

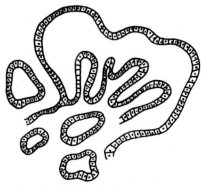

Low Grade (Grade1) Carcinoma:
composed of cells resembling normal
glandular cells. They form architecture
simulating a normal glandular structure
of the ovary.

High Grade (Grade3) Carcinoma:
composed of cells with highly abnormal
nuclei and its architecture has no
resemblance to normal glandular
structures of the ovary.

Common Epithelial Ovarian Cancers:
Pathologic Factors Associated with Survival

Better Long-Term Survival	Poorer Long-Term Survival
Grade 1 Well-Differentiated or Grade 2 Moderately Differentiated	Grade 3 Poorly Differentiated
Borderline Carcinoma/ Carcinomas of Low Malignant Potential	Frankly Malignant Carcinoma
Serous or Endometrioid Carcinomas	Clear-Cell Carcinoma

Chapter 6

The Four Stages of Ovarian Cancer: Stage and Survival

Dear Mr. Wilder:

Your story, Gilda's story, moved me in a very emotional, personal way. I did not know Gilda. I was not that familiar with "Saturday Night Live," but after learning of her illness and reading *It's Always Something,* I truly felt a closeness—and also a certain sadness that I could never have known such a wonderful human being.

Gilda's story has helped me so much, Mr. Wilder, because four and one-half years ago I was diagnosed with colon cancer. Though our cancers were different, I can remember feeling all the same fears, all the same emotions that Gilda speaks of in her book.

I was only forty-one years old and I can remember thinking that this cannot be, I am too young; there is no way I can possibly die. I began wondering about all of the things I had done in my life that could have caused this terrible disease to invade my body. Everything that Gilda questioned, I questioned; everything that talked of feeling, I felt. I gained so much from her story, Mr. Wilder; so much from her strengths, from her positive attitude, from her wonderful sense of humor—and two years after her death I am continuing to gain.

To continue this fight against ovarian cancer in Gilda's memory says so much about you.

Y. O.

On October 23, the internist did a pelvic, he checked Gilda into the hospital for tests and that night in the hospital she said, "At least somebody believes me." That night we were told that she had ovarian cancer and that they were going to operate. That was a Friday night and they were going to operate on Sunday morning. On Sunday morning, they took out a grapefruit-sized ovarian cancer. She had 3200 cc of fluid in her abdomen. For a while her doctors were very optimistic that she was going to be one of the lucky ones. But it came back, it is a very insidious disease, it was stage IV, not III, II, or I. She died on May 20, 1989.*

Like the phrase *get a second opinion*, the word *stage* has become part of our everyday lexicon when we think of cancer. Most people have a gut understanding that the higher the stage, the worse the outcome. And stage IV is the worst that one can have.

While it is true that stage IV is the the worst diagnosis, it is not true that all patients with stage IV ovarian cancer lose their battle with the disease. Regrettably, this was true for Gilda Radner. She was diagnosed with stage IV ovarian cancer, which had already spread to her bowel and liver, on October 20, 1986, nearly one year after her odyssey with every symptom *associated* with ovarian cancer began.

The stage of an ovarian cancer is determined by the location of the disease within the body. Is the cancer still confined within the ovary? Has it spread outside the ovary? And if it has spread outside the ovary, where has it gone?

---

*Gene Wilder, "Ovarian Cancer Familial Link?" A talk given at St. Luke's Medical Center, Milwaukee, Wisconsin, April 10, 1991.

Generally, stage I ovarian cancers are confined to the ovary; stage II cancers have spread outside the ovary but are still confined to the pelvic area (below the navel, or *belly button*); stage III cancers have spread above the navel to the abdomen; and stage IV cancers have progressed beyond the abdomen or have invaded the liver.

Stages I, II, and III are further subdivided as shown in the table developed by the International Federation of Gynecologists and Obstetricians (FIGO).* This table is used by your physician to indicate the progression of your disease. It's a little complicated, but it is important. Knowing the exact stage of your cancer guides your physician in determining the best treatment for you and can provide a gauge for assessing how well you are likely to respond to treatment.

STAGE I: THE OVARY

Twenty percent of all ovarian cancers are stage I. *True stage I* ovarian cancers have an encouraging 90 to 95 percent long-term survival rate. As usual, however, it's not that simple because not all stage I ovarian cancers are created equal.

For years, surgeons struggled to explain why the long-term survival rate remained so poor—under 70 percent—for tumors which at the time of surgery (for removal of the tumor and the uterus) appeared to be confined to the ovary. Research provided the explanation: Microscopic cancer cells were found to have escaped from the ovary and spread to other structures within the abdomen. These areas include the undersurface of the diaphragm (located just above the liver and nearly impossible to

---

*See Appendix, Table 6.1: "International Federation of Gynecologists and Obstetricians (FIGO) 1986 Staging for Ovarian Cancer."

reach through a bikini incision*), the omentum (a large area of fatty tissue attached to the upper part of the intestine), and the lymph nodes in the pelvic and abdominal regions.

True stage I ovarian cancers, therefore, can only be determined by a more extensive surgical procedure that not only removes the tumor and uterus, but also includes a sampling of cells from these other areas of the abdomen. It is only when these areas are sampled, evaluated microscopically by a pathologist, and found to contain no cancer cells that a patient has a true stage I cancer.

STAGE II: THE PELVIS

Stage II ovarian cancer is very rare, occurring in less than 10 percent of patients. The reason is that it would be unusual for cancer cells to break off the ovary and stay confined to an artificial boundary in the pelvic region below the belly button.

STAGES III AND IV:
THE ABDOMEN AND THE LIVER

"What I didn't know during this time in the hospital was that I didn't have just ovarian cancer. It had spread to my bowel and my liver, but the cells hadn't eaten into those organs. They were just lying on top of those organs, so the doctors had removed all the cancer they could see." (*It's Always Something*, p. 83)

---

*A bikini incision is a low transverse incision just above the pubic hair which would be parallel to the top of a bikini bathing suit.

Sixty percent of women diagnosed with ovarian cancer have stage III—the most common—and 10 percent are found to have stage IV disease. In fact, most ovarian cancer patients show signs of stage IIIC—tumor implants larger than $\frac{3}{4}$ of an inch (2 cm) within the abdomen—when first seen by their physicians.

However, it is the size of the tumor implants after surgery that predict the response to chemotherapy and long-term survival. We know that patients with stage III ovarian cancer do best when the surgeon is able to remove all the tumor and leave no tumor deposits in the pelvis or abdomen that are larger than $\frac{3}{8}$ of an inch (1 cm).

Therefore, if you are diagnosed with stage III ovarian cancer, what does it mean when your surgeon tells you after your operation that "the surgery went very well and I am hopeful"? It means that she or he took out as much of the cancer as possible and that no residual tumor deposits larger than $\frac{3}{8}$ of an inch (1 cm) were left behind. Intuitively, Gilda Radner understood this, when she wrote: "They were just lying on top of those organs, so the doctors had removed all the cancer they could see" (*It's Always Something,* p. 83).

SURVIVAL AFTER TREATMENT FOR OVARIAN CANCER

Survival figures for ovarian cancer or any type of cancer are always difficult to discuss, listen to, or even read about. Betty expressed it best in *It's Always Something.*

"Betty, one of the group leaders, said that if the statistics say that only 8 percent survive a particular cancer, no one knows who the 8 percent are. 'Every one of us has just as much right to be in the 8 percent as anybody else. If you

Figure 6.1

4 Stages of Ovarian Cancer

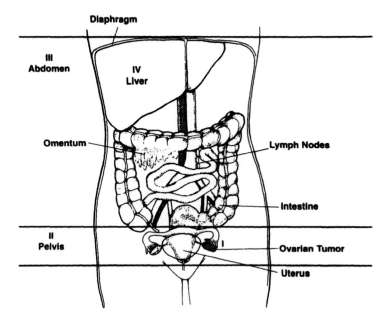

I   Confined to Ovary

II   Spread Outside of Ovary
Confined to Pelvis

III   Spread to Abdomen

IV   Spread to Liver or Beyond Abdomen

have cancer,' she said, 'do everything possible to fight it—
do any activity, any event, but participate in your recovery.' She was given only a 20 percent chance—eleven
years before. It seemed like the room began to stir with
hope." (*It's Always Something*, pp. 141–42)

Today, the five-year survival figures are: stage I, 90 to 95 percent; stage II, 70 to 80 percent; stage III, 20 to 30 percent; and
stage IV, 5 to 10 percent. Remember, these are just *averages*,
based on responses to current treatments. What might be the
best combination of drugs for ovarian cancer—taxol and Plati-
nol®—is so new that we must wait several years to see how much
these survival figures will improve. And they will!

"The internist told Gene that I had only a 20 percent
chance of survival and that they would not know until I
was two months into chemotherapy whether or not I
would survive. It depended entirely on whether I
responded to this particular chemotherapy. Gene, of
course, never told me, but he was carrying that information all the time behind his smiling face. Not surviving never
entered my head at all. Even today I feel so awful for
Gene that he was carrying that load and he couldn't let
on to me." (*It's Always Something*, pp. 83–84)

Chapter 7

Surgery of Ovarian Cancer: What Do I Need to Know?

Dear Mr. Wilder:

My reason for writing is to thank you personally for your efforts to help prevent other women from having the horrible experience that you and Gilda had. You may have saved my life. If I can help with this cause in any way as a volunteer, I would be happy to. Let me add that Gilda was adored by so many of us, and we were deeply moved when she died. You refer to her courage in your articles and I'm sure she was inspirational, but your own courage in continuing to focus attention to a devastating time in your life with Gilda for the benefit of others is remarkable as well.

You have my deepest sympathy, appreciation, and respect.

G. B.

It's always something! This is never more true than right before we perform major surgery for a suspected ovarian cancer. The problem is that we don't know, and we won't know until during surgery, exactly what we're dealing with, where it is located, and whether it has spread to other parts of the body. As illustrated in chapter 4, many sophisticated diagnostic tests have been developed over the years to help us; however, none has been able to distinguish a cancerous from a noncancerous pelvic mass. Only surgery and a biopsy of the tumor tissue will answer that.

For this reason, discussing surgery with a woman suspected of having ovarian cancer is never easy. Not knowing before surgery that the diagnosis is indeed ovarian cancer, our effectiveness is limited when it comes to preparing the patient mentally and emotionally for exactly what she can expect during the operation.

Contrast this with breast cancer, for example. While discussion of surgery with a woman suspected of having breast cancer is no easier, it can, in a sense, be more precise. In this case, the diagnosis of breast cancer is made by doing a biopsy of the suspected breast tumor. Once diagnosed and depending on the pathologist's findings, surgical options—lumpectomy (wide local excision of the tumor without removing the breast), mastectomy (removal of the entire breast), and possible lymph node removal (in the axilla or armpit)—can be discussed with the woman before surgery. In this way the patient usually has the time to evaluate the options and prepare herself emotionally for exactly what to expect during and after surgery.

In the case of ovarian cancer, the best we can do is to narrow to three the possible outcomes for women preparing for surgery: (1) a noncancerous pelvic mass, (2) ovarian cancer that appears to be confined to the ovary or pelvis, and (3) ovarian cancer that has spread to other organs.

Less than twenty years ago, when a woman was diagnosed with an ovarian cancer that appeared to the surgeon to be confined to the ovary, her uterus (hysterectomy), fallopian tubes, and ovaries were usually removed. Future treatment decisions relied on the ability of the surgeon to detect (and remove) areas of cancer. Sadly, even with this minimal amount of surgery for the *earliest* stage of ovarian cancer, only 70 percent of these patients survived for five years. Why?

(Above Left) Gilda's maternal grandmother, Goldie Dworkin: she died of "stomach cancer" on January 25, 1942. In those days, many ovarian cancers were referred to as stomach cancer, but we don't have a definite diagnosis. *(Above Right)* Gilda's maternal aunt Elsie Rhineston, who died of ovarian cancer. She is the mother of Lenore Goodman Rosa, Gilda's first cousin, who is a patient of Dr. Piver and who was treated for ovarian and breast cancer. *(Below Left)* Gilda's mother, who had breast cancer. *(Below Right)* Gilda's maternal aunt (Freda), who had no cancer. Photos courtesy of Lenore Goodman Rosa.

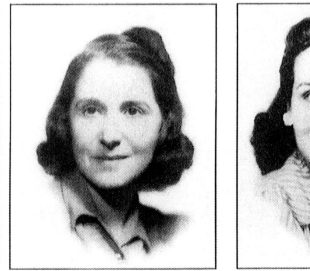

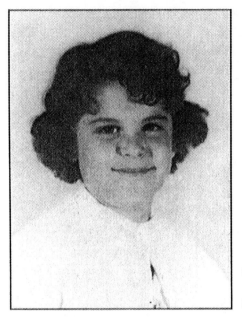

Gilda on her fifth birthday, 1951. She did tricks to steal the show even then.

Gilda Radner at a family get-together. Photo courtesy of Lenore Goodman Rosa.

Gilda as Roseanne Roseannadanna, 1978.

(Above) Gilda in Lenore's home in Detroit signing Roseanne Roseanna-danna photographs. *(Below)* Gilda's mother, her brother Michael, Gilda, and Lenore at the Renaissance Center in 1980 to celebrate her mother's seventy-fifth birthday. Photos courtesy of Lenore Goodman Rosa.

(Above) Gilda and Lenore at Gilda's mother's seventy-fifth birthday celebration. Photo courtesy of Lenore Goodman Rosa. *(Below)* Gilda and Gene in a publicity photo for the film *Haunted Honeymoon* (1984), before any signs or symptoms of cancer.

(Above) Gilda in 1987, after two chemotherapies, with a friend's three-month-old son. *(Below)* Gilda and Gene at the Special Olympics in 1988.

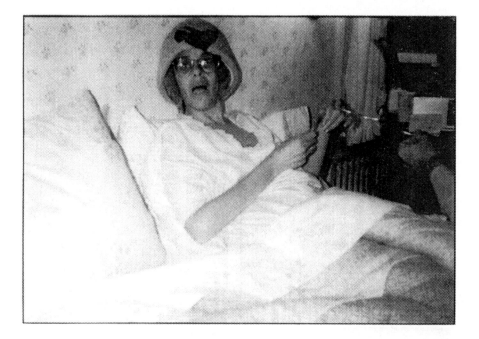

(Above) Gilda, wearing an ice pack to protect her hair, receiving chemotherapy at home in Connecticut, summer 1988. *(Below)* Gilda and Gene's last Christmas, 1988.

(Above) Gilda's first cousin Lenore Goodman Rosa in 1996. *(Right)* Lenore Goodman Rosa and her husband, Paul Rosa, in 1996. Photos courtesy of Lenore Goodman Rosa.

Today, removing as much of the cancer as possible seems to be a logical approach. But as recently as the 1970s, this logic escaped most surgeons. They often became discouraged at the time of surgery when confronted with widespread ovarian cancer and, just to confirm the diagnosis, they removed a biopsy sample from the most easily accessible tumor nodules as the only (the stress is on only) surgery.

Even sadder, during the 1970s and early 1980s, women found to have ovarian cancer widely spread in the abdomen usually had only a biopsy-sized piece of the tumor removed and no further surgery. Future treatment decisions for the cancer left behind were based on the pathologic evaluation of this sample. Only 5 percent of these women survived for five years. Was there a better way?

We needed answers and research has provided them. Today, we know that approaches such as *surgical staging* (systematic evaluation of the abdominal area) for early-staged ovarian cancer and *debulking surgery* (see pp. 103–107) for advanced-staged ovarian cancer are responsible for improving five-year survival rates for these women to 90 percent and between 20 and 25 percent, respectively. Remember, five years means *at least* five years. This magic number (five years) came about because it was believed that women who survived for five years after treatment for ovarian cancer were cured and that the cancer would not come back. As a general rule, this belief is confirmed. However, a very small percentage of women with ovarian cancer may still develop a recurrence five years after treatment. So, while the outlook for women has improved, it is still not good enough.

STAGES I AND II: WHY SURGICAL STAGING IS IMPORTANT

In 1978 answers to why only 70 percent of women with apparent stage I ovarian cancer survived five years started to become clear for the first time. That year, researchers were able to report a collective review of sites that ovarian cancer often spread to when the cancer appeared to the surgeon to be confined to the ovary. The cancer cells that had escaped from the ovary were microscopic and thus not visible to the surgeon.*

Surgeons were made aware that microscopic cancer cells may be present on the undersurface of the right diaphragm, in the omentum, in the lymph nodes along the abdominal aorta and pelvic cavity, and in the free-floating cells obtained by saline wash. They began to systematically evaluate these areas by abdominal *wash,* biopsy, or surgical removal, in a procedure that became known as *surgical staging.* Surgeons could now rely on the results of this surgical staging rather than visual inspection to accurately determine if the cancer was really confined to the ovary or pelvis, or if microscopic cancer cells had spread. Since then, surgical staging has guided future treatment decisions, which have improved five-year survival rates from 70 percent to 90 percent.

Do women facing ovarian cancer surgery really need to know about surgical staging? Yes! Women should be able to discuss surgical staging with their surgeon because it is so critically important in diagnosing the extent of their ovarian cancer and ensuring that effective treatment begins immediately.

The results of a study by the Ovarian Cancer Study Group† illustrate this. Surgeons reoperated on a hundred women within

---

*See Appendix, Table 7.1: "Incidence of Occult or Microscopic Metastases in Apparent Stage I or II Ovarian Cancer."

†Consisting of the National Cancer Institute, M. D. Anderson Tumor Institute, the Mayo Clinic, and Roswell Park Cancer Institute.

Figure 7.1

Surgical Staging

Stage I and Stage II Ovarian Cancer
5 Major Pathways of Spread

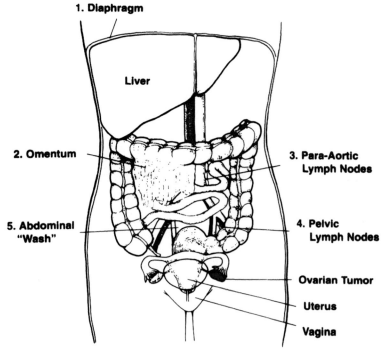

four weeks of their original surgery (performed without surgical staging) for presumed stage I and II ovarian cancer. On reoperation, this time with surgical staging, 31 percent (nearly one in three) were found to have unrecognized cancer metastases (i.e., a spread of cancer). In fact, 77 percent of these women were found actually to have stage III disease. For those women, the time for the most appropriate treatment may have been delayed until such treatment would no longer be helpful. Women with true stage I disease may have been treated unnecessarily. That is why surgical staging is important.

WHILE YOU WERE SLEEPING

Because you *will* be asleep (that is, under a general anesthetic), here are some questions and answers that describe briefly what your surgeon will be doing during surgery for possible early-staged ovarian cancer.

What Type of Incision Will Be Made?

The surgeon usually makes a vertical, midline incision from the pubic bone up to at least the belly button. This allows for careful evaluation of the upper abdomen, including the diaphragm.

What Happens after the Incision Is Made?

An *abdominal wash* is done by injecting a salt solution into the abdominal cavity. Why? We believe that ovarian cancer begins as a cystic growth within the ovary. Even when the capsule (outer covering) of the ovarian tumor is felt to be intact, tumor cells have the ability to penetrate or break through the capsule and shed into the abdominal cavity. To rule out this possibility, an abdominal *wash* is the first thing the surgeon does after the incision is made. Ovarian cancer cells later detected in the *wash* are not visible to the naked eye, but can be detected microscopically.

What Happens after the Abdominal Wash?

After the abdominal wash, the surgeon evaluates the pelvis and abdomen and then removes the suspected ovarian tumor. The ovarian tumor is sent to the pathologist for an immediate evaluation referred to as a *frozen section diagnosis*.

What Happens If the Frozen Section Diagnosis Is a Noncancerous Ovarian Tumor?

Depending on your age and your desire to retain your fertility, a hysterectomy and removal of the other fallopian tube and ovary may or may not be done.

What Happens If the Tumor Is Malignant, But Appears To Be Confined to the Ovary?

Again, this depends on the grade (see chapter 5) of the tumor and your desire to retain your fertility. If you are young and want to retain your fertility, and the ovarian cancer is a borderline or grade 1 tumor, the other tube and ovary will be inspected very carefully and, if normal, the tube, ovary, and uterus will not be removed. However, meticulous surgical staging will be carried out. For almost all other ovarian cancers, the other tube and ovary and the uterus will be removed.

What Does Meticulous Surgical Staging Involve?

After the abdominal wash and the diagnosis of ovarian cancer is confirmed by frozen section diagnosis, *surgical staging* begins with an evaluation of the undersurface of the diaphragm for possible tumor cells. Why? The undersurface of the right side of the diaphragm is a frequent site of microscopic ovarian cancer cells even in the early stages of the disease. Because of the normal respiratory motion of the diaphragm and the movement of the intestines, any free-floating tumor cells that have broken through the ovarian tumor capsule will be moved through the abdominal cavity in a clockwise rotation (which is the normal movement of the intestines) and can implant on the undersurface of the right side of the diaphragm.

Next comes the removal of the omentum, referred to technically as an *omentectomy*. The omentum is a fatty piece of tissue attached to the upper portion of the colon. The omentum has a *carpet sweeper* action that captures tumor cells as they move through the abdominal cavity.

The pelvic lymph nodes (along the pelvis) and the paraaortic lymph nodes (along the lower abdominal aorta) often harbor microscopic ovarian cancer cells that have spread to the abdominal cavity. These are removed next.

To reemphasize, some 30 percent of women who undergo this meticulous surgical staging for presumed stage I ovarian cancer will have microscopic metastasis to one of these five areas. The good news is that for those women who are found to have true stage I ovarian cancer, the long-term survival is 90 to 95 percent, and, just as important, they may not require postoperative chemotherapy.

A Final Thought on Surgical Staging

Researchers from George Washington University examined the completeness of surgical staging in 291 women with ovarian cancer. They found that surgical staging by gynecologic oncologists was performed properly in 97 percent of cases. However, surgical staging by obstetricians and gynecologists was performed properly in only 52 percent of cases and by general surgeons in only 35 percent of cases. It is now known that only about 25 percent of women in the United States with ovarian cancer are operated on by gynecologic oncologists.

STAGES III AND IV: WHY AGGRESSIVE ("DEBULKING") SURGERY IS IMPORTANT

"My surgery involved a total hysterectomy. I would never have a baby. Everything had happened so fast. I hadn't even realized before the operation that it would probably involve the removal of my reproductive organs. When they told me afterward, I understood the issue was to save my life. There was nothing to say. No more biological clock to worry about. The important thing was that I was alive. . . .

"I spent three weeks in the hospital. Although I had major surgery for the removal of a grapefruit-sized tumor, a complete hysterectomy and a scraping of many of my internal organs, I spent the first week out of intensive care in the dreamy state of happiness. . . ." (*It's Always Something*, pp. 74, 76)

The *unknowns* before surgery for presumed advanced-staged ovarian cancer are pretty much the same as those for early-staged ovarian cancer. Gilda Radner's case was unusual. She knew she had a malignancy before surgery, because as she wrote: "On Friday (October 23, 1986), fluid was extracted from my swollen belly." Advanced-staged ovarian cancer often causes a buildup of fluid in the abdomen (ascites). This fluid causes the characteristic abdominal distention, which Gilda characterized as "clothes that don't fit," and often contains free-floating cancer cells. However, neither Gilda nor her doctors knew whether it was ovarian cancer or the extent of surgery that would be required.

Gilda's response to being told that a malignancy had been discovered was "No more bad news, no more bad news, please! I just don't want any more bad news."

"I can't remember much after that. I don't remember being horrified or dwelling on it—whether it was because they were medicating me at that point, I don't know. Everything happened quickly from that Friday night until they operated on me Sunday morning. Saturday I was prepped for surgery and Gene says I met the anesthesiologist and the gynecologist who was to perform the operation. I don't remember anything. I was probably filled with medication that dripped through my intravenous line. I do remember that nobody said the word *cancer*." (*It's Always Something*, p. 73)

In most women suspected of having advanced-staged ovarian cancer, the presurgery discussions should focus on the need for a clearer diagnosis to determine if it is an advanced ovarian cancer, and to remove as much of the tumor and tumor deposits as possible.

Successful debulking surgery can result in only $\frac{1}{1,000}$ of the original tumor cell population remaining after surgery. The scientific rationale of what we now know—that small tumors respond better than large tumors to chemotherapy—is that removing large tumors before chemotherapy can remove cancer cells that may have already developed resistance to chemotherapy, just as some bacterial throat infections develop resistance to penicillin or other antibiotics. Also, large tumors outgrow the blood supply required to nourish them, and to deliver chemotherapy. Thus, debulking the tumor down to small tumors improves the blood supply and the chance that chemotherapy will actually reach the tumor.

The logic of this surgical approach escaped *no one* following a 1978 report by researchers at Harvard that fathered the concept of debulking (cytoreductive) surgery. Their study found that the size of the tumor deposits in the abdomen was the key to long-term survival for patients with stage III and IV ovarian cancer. They reported the same long-term survival for two groups of such patients with tumor deposits in the abdomen that measured $\frac{5}{8}$ of an inch (1.5 cm) or smaller. What distinguished the two groups was that in one group the tumor deposits were discovered at the time the surgeon entered the abdominal cavity and removed them, and in the other group the deposits were left behind after the surgeon removed as much of the ovarian cancer tumor as possible. In contrast to these two groups of patients, no patient survived if tumor deposits larger than $\frac{5}{8}$ of an inch were left behind.

At about this same time, positive results of research on the effectiveness of Platinol® chemotherapy in curing even widespread ovarian cancer were being reported. The intensity and frustration of years of research were beginning to pay dividends. Doctors now had the tools to give new hope to patients with advanced-staged ovarian cancer.

In preparing the patient for surgery, the surgeon must explain that if the diagnosis of ovarian cancer is confirmed, the goal will be to remove any and hopefully all tumor deposits located outside the ovary, and not to leave behind any deposits larger than $\frac{3}{8}$ of an inch (1 cm) (even smaller than the original size of $\frac{5}{8}$ of an inch or 1.5 cm reported by the Harvard research team). To achieve this goal, the surgeon may have to remove a small portion of the intestine. In fact, a study at Roswell Park Cancer Institute found that 36 percent of the patients studied required some type of intestinal surgery. This possibility should, of course, be discussed in advance of the surgery.*

Patients who have successful debulking surgery (no residual tumor deposits larger than ⅜ of an inch [1 cm]) followed by Platinol® chemotherapy have the best chance for long-term survival. This was confirmed in a 1994 study at Roswell Park Cancer Institute of 136 patients treated with Platinol® after surgery. The five-year survival rate was 50 percent for those with tumor deposits after surgery less than or equal to ⅜ of an inch (1 cm). This decreased dramatically to 19 percent for those with tumor deposits between ⅜ and ¾ of an inch (1 and 2 cm), and to 13 percent for those with tumor deposits larger than ¾ of an inch (2 cm).†

A Final Thought on Debulking Surgery

The purpose of debulking surgery is to render the operation potentially curative. The opinion may be best expressed in an editorial in the *British Journal of Surgery*:

> Therefore, in addition to *hysterectomy* [removal of the uterus], *salpingo-oophorectomy* [removal of the fallopian tubes and ovaries] and *omentectomy* [removal of the omentum], a technical and demanding intestinal resection may be necessary in up to 40 percent of patients for adequate debulking of advanced ovarian cancer. Who should be performing this extensive cytoreductive surgery with minimal patient morbidity rates? It

---

*See Appendix, Table 7.2: "Surgery for Stage III and IV Ovarian Cancer."

†See Appendix, Figure 1: "Long-Term Survival by Cytoreductive Surgery . . ."

must be a surgeon who regularly performs the necessary surgical techniques, particularly resection and restoration of colorectal continuity. In an ideal world, this would be a suitably trained and experienced gynecologic oncologist.*

Having described the various surgical procedures, and the importance of surgical staging, for ovarian cancer, let us now move on to the kinds of chemotherapy available to combat this disease: their benefits, limits, and side effects.

---

*N. A. Scott and P. F. Schofield, "Cytoreductive Surgery for Ovarian Carcinoma," *British Journal of Surgery* 77 (1990): 481–82.

Chapter 8

First-Line Chemotherapy of Ovarian Cancer

Dear Mr. Wilder:

I've wanted to write you for some time. I need to share with you the way Gilda touched my life. In 1979, I was fifteen, suicidal, confused. I was abused by an older sister and felt alone. I had just quit school, my self-esteem was low, everyone told me how I felt and what I wanted. I was shy but blossomed on stage, yet I was not popular enough to be cast in a high school play. It was during this time the local college held auditions for a parody of "Saturday Night Live." The roles of Gilda's characters were precast. But she was my favorite on the show and I challenged them and won. I played her characters to an overstuffed audience for three nights (three wonderful nights).

That's how Gilda inspired me. I've been active in theater since. It's wonderful that lives can be touched in positive ways, even unawaredly. I had pictures of her characters. They always give me a boost—they remind me of transformations and how we touch everything, even strangers. I remember I was driving some handicapped clients when I heard Gilda passed over. My heart dropped. Still, when I watch her on video, I feel sad, joy and gratitude. I hope this letter reaches you—it can—I believe. The work she gave you is a blessing.

My mother and I are both fighting off different cancers. I believe awareness and action keeps my condition minimal.

Thank you for spreading the light of awareness and I thank Gilda for the healing strength and humor.

V. S.

A SHORT HISTORY

"In the hospital I was told that I was to have nine sessions of chemotherapy spaced approximately three weeks apart and involving two major chemicals, called cisplatin and Cytoxan. The number of treatments had been determined through experimentation that is constantly being revised. With only six sessions there was recurrence of cancer, and with twelve the side effects became too severe. I had my first treatment before I left the hospital. So not only was I coming home as someone recovering from major surgery, but I had just been zapped with chemicals to kill any cancer that was left in my body. That's all the dreaded 'chemo' treatment really is: doses of chemicals—drugs, medications—administered intravenously or in shots or in pills that have been found to kill cancer cells. Of course, a lot of healthy cells get knocked around in the process, causing side effects like hair loss, nausea, fatigue and lowered blood counts, but the healthy cells regenerate. The hope is that the cancer cells won't. . . .

"As the month following the last chemo went by, my strength returned. I could taste wellness. I felt so well that I got depressed because I had to go into the hospital again. I also found that I was angry about the whole sec-

ond-look surgery. There I was in what I had hoped would
be the last steps of this cancer, but I hated that I had to
take a couple of steps backward in order to go forward
again." (*It's Always Something,* pp. 106, 180–81)

Today, most women who receive chemotherapy following
surgery for ovarian cancer receive two drugs—taxol and
Platinol.® This is referred to as *first-line* chemotherapy because it
is the first chemotherapy given after surgery, and because it consists of drugs which research has shown to be the most effective
available for treating ovarian cancer.

When I treated my first patient in the summer of 1968, the
only chemotherapy available was Melphalan® and similar alkylating chemotherapy agents. At that time, women survived an average of only eight months. Today, with taxol and Platinol®, women
are surviving an average of thirty-eight months. While this 375
percent improvement is a good start, it is only a start!

You may find it interesting to learn how we arrived at this
point in the history of chemotherapy.

Using drugs to treat cancer began literally by accident—a
tragic accident. During World War II, nitrogen mustard gas
exploded aboard a submarine, and when the sailors who were
exposed became ill, they were found to have had most of their
white blood cells destroyed. This medical news fueled the imagination of doctors treating patients who had leukemia. Because
leukemia is characterized by too many abnormal white blood
cells, they wondered if nitrogen mustard could effectively destroy
these white blood cells. The glimmer of hope from the early
results intensified research on chemotherapy for cancer.

The first success with chemotherapy for ovarian cancer came
in 1952. Hemisulfide mustard (an alkylating agent closely related
to nitrogen mustard) was found to control the fluid buildup
within the abdomen of women with advanced ovarian cancer. In
1962, researchers at the M. D. Anderson Tumor Institute in Houston, Texas, reported the first successful use of another alkylating

agent related to nitrogen mustard, phenylalanine mustard (Melphalan®). This agent significantly reduced the size of the tumors.

The first indication Melphalan® could actually cure women with ovarian cancer came in 1966 when researchers from the M. D. Anderson Tumor Institute reported positive results on thirteen patients with advanced ovarian cancer (chapter 9). However, along with this giant step forward came the realization that if these alkylating agents did not control the growth of ovarian cancer, there were no other real options. A new drug or combination of drugs was needed.

Serendipity was also involved in the discovery of the most important drug for ovarian cancer—Platinol®, another type of alkylating agent. In 1965, researcher Barnett Rosenberg was not searching for a new chemical for treating cancer, but instead he was testing bacteria to determine the effects of electrical fields on growing cells. To his surprise, the cells in the bacteria stopped dividing. This effect was attributed to a platinum compound that had separated from the platinum electrodes. This discovery of Platinol® gave birth to the modern era of chemotherapy for ovarian cancer. By 1976, researchers from the United Kingdom had reported the first results showing that Platinol® significantly reduced the size of ovarian tumors that had failed to respond to other alkylating agents.

If Melphalan® was the drug of the 1970s and Platinol® the drug of the 1980s, then taxol has become the drug of the 1990s. Although taxol was discovered in the 1960s from extracts of the bark of the Pacific Yew tree, it was not until 1989 that researchers from Johns Hopkins University reported that taxol was effective in shrinking ovarian tumors in 30 percent of women who had not responded to Platinol® chemotherapy. These responses lasted from three to fifteen months. The next obvious step was to combine taxol and Platinol® as first-line chemotherapy. More on this later in this chapter.

BACK TO BASICS

What Does Chemotherapy Do?

Cancer cells divide rapidly to reproduce themselves. Chemotherapy kills cancer cells by disrupting their ability to divide and reproduce. The bad news is that chemotherapy may also destroy or harm many of the normal cells in the body which also divide rapidly—red blood cells (RBCs), white blood cells (WBCs), platelets, hair cells, and cells lining the digestive tract from the mouth to the anus. Cells most vulnerable initially to chemotherapy are RBCs, which are needed to carry oxygen to tissues; WBCs, which are needed to help fight infections; and platelets, which are required for blood to clot. Since ovarian cancer almost never involves the bone marrow where RBCs, WBCs, and platelets are made, the body is able to replenish these important cells, usually between courses of chemotherapy. (See Figure 8.1, which illustrates normal cell division.)

How Does Chemotherapy Work?

Different classes of chemotherapy drugs act at different points during the cell cycle of the cancer cell. Usually, more than two different classes of drugs are given to capitalize on these different points of attack and to maximize the ability of the drugs to destroy cancer cells. Combining two or more chemotherapy drugs also helps prevent cancer cells from becoming resistant to the individual drugs.

A course of chemotherapy does not kill a specific number of cancer cells, but rather kills a constant fraction of cancer cells

Figure 8.1

Cell Cycle

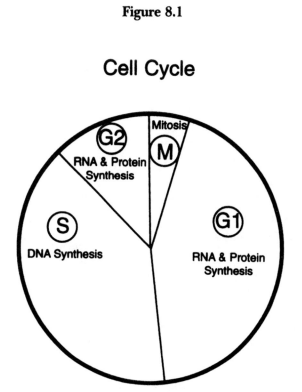

During normal cell division, cells proceed through different phases. During the G1 phase of the cell cycle, enzymes that are essential for the production of RNA (ribonucleic acid) and protein, the building blocks of all cells, are produced. In preparation for cell division during the S phase, DNA (deoxyribonucleic acid) is synthesized by replication of the existing strand to produce a copy. RNA and protein are synthesized during the G2 phase. During M phase the four stages of mitosis occur: prophase, metaphase, anaphase, and telophase. Cell division during mitosis results in two daughter cells, each of which can enter the G1 phase of the cell cycle.

during each course. For example, one drug will destroy a certain fraction of cancer cells (let's say 90 percent), and the second drug destroys a similar fraction (again, let's say 90 percent) of the remaining cancer cells. The result is that the combination destroys a higher fraction of cancer cells with each course of chemotherapy. Because each course of chemotherapy destroys a constant fraction of remaining cancer cells, there should come a point when 99.9999 percent of the cancer cells will be killed, allowing the body's immune system to eradicate the remaining .0001 percent.

Chemotherapy is administered every twenty-one to twenty-eight days to give the body time to replace the normal cells—RBCs, WBCs, and platelets—before any new ovarian cancer cells can grow. Any longer delay between treatments would allow both normal and cancer cells to reproduce.

CLASSES OF CHEMOTHERAPY DRUGS

Alkylating Agents

Melphalan®, Cytoxan, Platinol®, Carboplatin, Ifosfamide, and Thiotepa are alkylating agents used to treat ovarian cancer. These agents bind with the DNA of the cancer cells and prevent them from dividing and reproducing.

Drugs Derived from Natural Plant Products

Taxol—the most important of these drugs—works like no other type of chemotherapy, in that it paralyzes cancer cells during cell division, but does not destroy them. Instead, other mechanisms kill the cancer cells while they are paralyzed. Etoposide (VP-16) is another example of a paralyzing cancer drug derived from natural plant products.

Antitumor Antibiotics

Adriamycin and Mitoxantrone are two commonly used antitumor antibiotics. These drugs also bind to DNA to prevent cell division.

Antimetabolites

Antimetabolites—e.g., 5-Fluorouracil, Methotrexate, and Cytarabine—are used rarely in ovarian cancer. These drugs trick cancer cells into believing they are normal metabolites, which are required by all cells. Because they appear normal, cancer cells pick up these antimetabolites and die because they are deprived of the normal metabolites they need to reproduce.

Miscellaneous Drugs

Hexamethylmelamine (Hexalin) is the only drug in this category used in ovarian cancer. It inhibits the incorporation of precursors into DNA and RNA (ribonucleic acid) and therefore inhibits DNA.

THE STORY OF PLATINOL® AND TAXOL

How Are Taxol and Platinol® Given?

Taxol and Platinol® are administered into a vein in the arm (peripheral IVs) and allowed to drip into the bloodstream by gravity. The bloodstream carries the drugs to the ovarian tumor. Taxol is given first—over a 24-hour period—because research has shown that doing so significantly reduces side effects. But first, because some women have had allergic reactions to taxol, a steroid (Decadron) and usually two histamines (Benadryl and Zantac) are given either orally or intravenously to prevent these. Following taxol, diuretics are given and then Platinol® is administered over a six- to eight-hour period.

Women whose veins are difficult to find can receive their chemotherapy through one of two special types of catheter known as central venous catheters. One type—e.g., Hickman and Groshong catheters—are tunneled beneath the skin and inserted into either a vein in the arm or a major vein in the neck area. The other end is visible on the outside of the arm or the chest wall. Port catheters—Mediports and Port-a-caths—are the other type of central venous catheter used. These are also inserted into a vein in the arm or neck area, but they are completely beneath the skin. They have a small plastic or metal port stitched just under the skin surface which is connected to the catheter. A small needle is injected through the skin into this port to give chemotherapy (see Figure 8.2).

Both types of catheters require monthly cleaning.

Figure 8.2

Intravenous Chemotherapy
Peripheral or Central Port

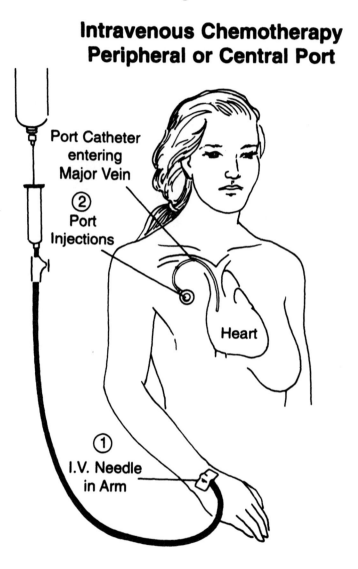

This figure illustrates two main methods of delivering chemotherapy:
(1) through intravenous (IV) in the arm and (2) through a central catheter port which has been surgically placed beneath the skin.

Side Effects of Taxol Chemotherapy

Decreased White Blood Counts

The normal WBC count ranges from 4,000 to 11,000. A decreased WBC count following taxol chemotherapy most often occurs six to eight days after each course of chemotherapy, reaches its lowest count (nadir) between days eight and eleven, and rebounds to near normal between days fifteen and twenty-one. When the WBC count falls below 1,000, the body's immune system is less able to fight infection. Antibiotics are often prescribed at this time to prevent infection until the WBC count returns to more than 1,000 and all cultures (blood, urine, etc.) contain no sign of infection. Neutrophils, which help fight infection, are a specific type of WBC. When the neutrophil level falls below 500—a condition known as *neutropenia*—antibiotics are almost always given to help prevent infection.

Colony-stimulating factors may be injected when the WBC count becomes dangerously low. These biological agents stimulate the bone marrow to reproduce WBCs at a faster pace so that neutropenia does not become worse and last as long. The most common of these agents—G-CSF and GM-CSF—may have mild side effects. G-CSF can cause bone pain and GM-CSF flu-like symptoms: fever, chills, malaise, and bone pain. Tylenol almost always relieves these side effects.

Reduced Number of Platelets

The normal platelet (clotting cell) count is more than 100,000. There is usually no concern until the count falls below 50,000, a condition known as *thrombocytopenia*. Patients with this condition may notice unexplained skin bruises, nose bleeds, or other signs of bleeding. Platelet counts below 20,000 can be dangerous and often require platelet transfusions to help the blood to clot while the bone marrow is producing more platelets. There are no colony-stimulating factors to induce the bone marrow to produce platelets.

Decreased Red Blood Cell Count

Hemoglobin is the component of RBCs that carries oxygen to other tissues in the body. The normal hemoglobin count is from twelve to sixteen grams. When hemoglobin levels fall below eight grams—a condition known as *anemia*—the patient feels tired and short of breath. Blood transfusions are usually required. The colony-stimulating factor, erythropoietin (Procit), can be used to prevent anemia.

Peripheral Neuropathy

Taxol may damage the nerves, primarily in the hands and feet, resulting in numbness and tingling (parasthesia). Severe symptoms occur in only 3 percent of women. Most mild symptoms subside within several months after treatment with taxol.

Slow Heart Beat (Bradycardia) or Irregular Heart Beat (Arrhythmia)

About 3 percent of women treated with taxol will develop a slowing of their heart rate which usually does not cause symptoms. Less than 1 percent of women develop serious irregular heart beat.

Digestive Tract

"... But eating was very unpleasant. I craved salty things because I could taste them. I ate what I ordinarily wouldn't eat. I wanted cheeseburgers, cheese and pickles. Lettuce and vegetables tasted like plastic. The highly salty, tasty things were good, but bland foods tasted like something they weren't, and that was too strange. It was too weird when a carrot tasted like a ceramic kitchen magnet." (*It's Always Something,* p. 114)

Taxol can cause nausea and vomiting but, unlike with many other chemotherapy drugs, attacks are rarely severe. A new class of drug, Zofran (Ondansetron), has completely changed the treatment of severe nausea and vomiting. Giving Zofran intravenously just before and several hours after chemotherapy has eliminated nausea and vomiting in 90 percent of women receiving chemotherapy for ovarian cancer. Chemotherapy may leave a funny or metallic taste in the mouth and may cause an aversion to food. Taxol (unlike 5-Fluorouracil) very rarely causes mouth sores (stomatitis) or severe diarrhea.

Hair Loss (Alopecia)

Because hair cells are also rapidly dividing cells, 90 percent of women treated with taxol will lose almost all of their hair. Taxol also affects the eyelashes, eyebrows, underarm hair, and pubic hair. Hair loss begins two to three weeks after the first treatment. Most women purchase a wig at the beginning of their treatment to match their normal hair style and color. But women should not lose heart. The hair usually (but not always) grows back, and sometimes thicker than ever.

Fatigue

Most women feel fatigued after completing a course of taxol chemotherapy, especially for the first few days. This fatigue usually lasts for a short time and subsides with each successive treatment.

Side Effects of Platinol® Chemotherapy

Platinol, like taxol, can cause neutropenia, thrombocytopenia, anemia, peripheral neuropathy, nausea, vomiting, diarrhea, and stomatitis (rarely). Unlike taxol, Platinol® almost never causes a slowing of the heart, irregular heart beat, or hair loss.

The major difference between taxol and Platinol® is the possible damage Platinol® can do to the kidneys. However, researchers have discovered that most moderate to severe kidney damage can be prevented by giving intravenous fluids (hydration) and diuretics (drugs that promote the excretion of urine) before Platinol® and administering Platinol® over a six- to eight-hour period. Kidney damage is monitored by measuring the blood urea nitrogen (BUN) and blood creatinine levels, both of which are measures of how well the kidneys are functioning.

Measuring the Effectiveness of Chemotherapy

The CA125 blood test and CT (computed tomography) scan of the pelvis and abdomen (see chapter 4) are two methods used during the course of chemotherapy to measure its effectiveness. A CA125 level that is falling toward normal (less than 35 units) indicates that the treatment is effective in destroying cancer cells.

Women whose CA125 returns to normal after the first three cycles of Platinol® chemotherapy are significantly less likely to have evidence of persistent ovarian cancer at second-look surgery.*

If physical examination or CT scan of the pelvis and abdomen indicates that any tumors or tumor deposits are still present after surgery, the effectiveness of chemotherapy is measured by the reduction in size of these residual tumors. For example, a 50 percent decrease in size is considered a partial response. A 100 percent regression in the size of the tumor is considered a complete response.

RESULTS OF CHEMOTHERAPY IN OVARIAN CANCER

This is essentially another short history, but this time concerning the results of early studies on chemotherapy for ovarian cancer. These studies have been the building blocks for a succession of more effective therapies and have increased the medical community's enthusiasm for the combination of taxol and Platinol®, at least for today.

A note before we begin. Thus far, we have referred to *five-year survival rates* for the most part. The results of some of the studies presented here are expressed in terms of the *disease-free survival rate,* so it would be a good time to explain the difference. Five-year survival rates tell us the percentage of women who have actually survived for at least five years after their initial treatment for ovarian cancer. But that's not the whole story! These percentages include women whose ovarian cancer has recurred after initial treatment, indicating that their treatment was not completely successful, but that they still survived for at least five years. The true value of any treatment is the percentage of

---

*See Appendix, Table 4.3: "CA125 Levels and Response to Therapy for Ovarian Cancer."

women surviving for at least five years without suffering a recurrence of their ovarian cancer. This is referred to as the *five-year disease-free survival rate.*

Stage I

A 1990 study by members of the Ovarian Cancer Study Group and the Gynecologic Oncology Group reported the only solid evidence that some women with ovarian cancer do not require chemotherapy after surgery. Women with stage IA* and B† (chapter 6), grade 1 ovarian cancer‡ (chapter 5) were randomly assigned to receive either six months of Melphalan® or no further treatment. The five-year survival rate for women receiving no further treatment was 92 percent, essentially the same as the 95 percent five-year survival rate for those treated with Melphalan®.

In another study done in 1995, researchers in Italy (the Gruppo Interregionale Collaborativo in Ginecologia Oncologica) randomly assigned women with stage I, grades 2 and 3, and stage IC (cancer cells in the abdominal washings) ovarian cancer to receive either Platinol® chemotherapy or no further treatment. In this study, the women receiving Platinol® had a five-year disease-free survival rate of 83 percent, compared to only 65 percent for women who received no further treatment.

In summary, women with stage I, grade 1 ovarian cancer have an excellent (greater than 90 percent) disease-free survival rate, and additional therapy after surgery has not been shown to be beneficial. Platinol® chemotherapy has been shown to be effective first-line chemotherapy for women with stage I, grades 2**

---

*Involvement of one ovary only.
†Involvement of two ovaries only.
‡Well-differentiated ovarian adenocarcinoma.
**Moderately differentiated ovarian adenocarcinoma.

and 3,* and stage IC ovarian cancer, and the results can be expected to be even better with the addition of taxol.

Stage II

A second study done in 1987 by members of the Ovarian Cancer Study Group and the Gynecologic Oncology Group was in patients with stage II ovarian cancer who had undergone complete surgical staging. These women were randomly assigned to receive either Melphalan® or the radioactive chemical P32 administered into the abdomen. About one-third of the patients in both groups developed a recurrent ovarian cancer. The two treatments resulted in essentially the same five-year survival rate of only 74 percent.

While there have been no large studies to evaluate the combination of taxol and Platinol® in women with stage II ovarian cancer, researchers hope that its effectiveness in these patients can be predicted from the results using these drugs in women with more advanced stage III and IV disease.

Stages III and IV

Taxol and Platinol® have recently become the *gold standard* treatment for advanced ovarian cancer, based on a report by the Gynecologic Oncology Group.† All women in this study had stage III or IV ovarian cancer and residual tumors after initial

---

*Poorly differentiated ovarian adenocarcinoma.

†W. P. McGuire, W. J. Hoskins, W. F. Brady, et al., "Cyclophosphamide and Cisplatin in Patients with Stage III and Stage IV Ovarian Cancer," *New England Journal of Medicine* 334 (1996): 1–6.

surgery measuring ⅜ of an inch (1 cm) or larger. You'll remember from chapter 7 that the best response rates and five-year survival rates are possible in women treated with chemotherapy for residual tumors after surgery measuring less than ⅜ of an inch (1 cm). Therefore, while the results of this study are encouraging, we can expect that taxol and Platinol® will be even more effective in this patient population.

In this study, women were assigned to receive either Platinol® and Cytoxan or taxol and Platinol®. Taxol was administered over a twenty-four-hour period, followed by Platinol® over a six-hour period the second day. Cytoxan is administered over thirty minutes. The measurable responses (complete and partial) were 73 percent for the taxol/Platinol® group and 60 percent for the Platinol®/Cytoxan group. More importantly, women in the taxol/Platinol® group survived an average of three years (thirty-eight months) compared to two years for women in the Platinol®/Cytoxan group. The taxol/Platinol® group also experienced an average increase in disease-free survival of eighteen months, compared to thirteen months for the Platinol®/Cytoxan group.

A FINAL NOTE

Taxol and Platinol® represent the best first-line chemotherapy treatment available today. Hopefully, this is another building block for better and improved treatments of tomorrow. But we still have to do better.

Chapter 9

Second-Look Surgery

Dear Mr. Wilder:

Although I cannot put it into words, I felt a great sadness when Gilda died. When I was in high school, my friends and I would watch "Saturday Night Live" every week. Being a teenager was sometimes tough, but being able to laugh with her every week made teenage life much more enjoyable. My ten-year high school reunion is in November, and we will be remembering Gilda in our program.

I guess part of the reason I am writing is to thank you on behalf of all the women's lives you will save with your awareness program. I believe that every person on this earth has a reason and a purpose for being here. Gilda's life was spent making people laugh, but her passing has a much greater purpose.

Gilda will be remembered at our high school reunion, but she will forever have a special place in my heart. She made me laugh when I needed it most.

Gilda made this world a better place.

V. L. K.

"Wouldn't you know that I would have the kind of cancer where they have to open you up again? With most cancers, you go through your course of chemo and then you just have to believe that it worked and killed all the cancer cells. I had to have an opening, a second opening, a big show, where they could look in and see, putting a whole lot of opening-night pressure on a very tired Gilda. . . ." (*It's Always Something*, p. 180)

Gilda's words tell us that the many months of treatment and uncertainty were taking their toll emotionally as well as physically. Her anger, depression, and frustration, when facing yet another procedure, were clear. Gilda was tired and tired of it. This isn't unusual. These feelings often supplant the "I'm going to beat this" attitude expressed by most patients immediately after diagnosis. Communication is often an early victim at this time, misunderstandings often the result. This appears to be true from Gilda's view of second-look surgery.

PROS AND CONS

What Second-Look Surgery (Laparotomy) Is and Is Not

As with any topic shrouded by misconception, it is important to define exactly what second-look surgery, referred to as *second-look laparotomy*, is and what it is not.

First, ovarian cancer is not the type of cancer in which they *have* to open you up again. In fact, the reason surgeons began performing second-look laparotomy fifty years ago had nothing to do with ovarian cancer. More on that later, under "A Brief History." On the other hand, if the physician wants to be as certain as possible that there is no remaining ovarian cancer, then sec-

ond-look surgery may be beneficial. The emphasis here is on *may
be beneficial.*

Second-look laparotomy is an exploratory procedure performed *only* after a woman with ovarian cancer has completed
her prescribed course of chemotherapy and has no evidence of
persistent cancer on examination by her physician or by X-ray
examination.

Now that you know what it *is,* let me point out a few things
that second-look laparotomy *is not.* Second-look laparotomy is
not a second operation for women with evidence of persistent
ovarian cancer after completing their prescribed chemotherapy;
nor for women with cancer that has progressed during their prescribed chemotherapy; nor for women treated previously who
now have evidence of recurrence. Also, second-look laparotomy
is *not* usually a second operation for women with stage I ovarian
cancer. It all depends on whether meticulous surgical staging
(see chapter 7) was done during the original operation. In
women who have had initial meticulous surgical staging, the likelihood of finding persistent ovarian cancer on second-look
laparotomy is only 5 percent. However, this likelihood increases
to 20 percent in those patients who did not have initial meticulous surgical staging.

A Brief History

The concept of a second-look laparotomy to evaluate the status
of a patient's cancer was introduced almost fifty years ago in
patients with colon cancer. This was before the era of effective
chemotherapy for cancer, and was the only method physicians
had to determine if cancer was still present and, if it was, if it
could be removed.

The impetus for a second-look laparotomy in patients with
ovarian cancer occurred in 1966. Researchers at the M. D.

Anderson Tumor Institute reported on thirteen patients with ovarian cancer who had truly amazing findings. These thirteen patients had such an unusually good response to Melphalan® chemotherapy (remember, this was thirty years ago) that a second-look laparotomy was performed to determine if an inoperable tumor had become removable and to evaluate the need for additional therapy. In each of the thirteen patients, to the amazement of the surgeon, no tumor was found and chemotherapy was discontinued. Not only was this the beginning of second-look laparotomy in advanced ovarian cancer, but it was the first realization that chemotherapy could be curative and not just palliative for women with ovarian cancer.

However, this very good news was followed by some not-so-good news. At that time, alkylating agents were the drugs used to treat ovarian cancer. Unfortunately, very few women were cured, and those who did survive often received chemotherapy for years. In the 1970s and early 1980s, a small percentage of women who had survived ovarian cancer as a result of long-term treatment with alkylating agents, developed leukemia. Second-look laparotomy became even more important because if no cancer was detected during the procedure, the physician could discontinue chemotherapy before leukemia developed.*

By the 1980s, Platinol®, a new alkylating agent, had been extensively tested on women with ovarian cancer. Platinol® chemotherapy was more effective and more convenient: the required number of courses could be administered over six months rather than over years, dramatically reducing the risk of leukemia from long-term chemotherapy. The effectiveness of Platinol® chemotherapy, plus a lack of subsequent treatment options that might have resulted in cure, made the use of second-look laparotomy controversial.

---

*M. S. Piver, "Ovarian Carcinoma: A Decade of Progress," *Cancer* 54 (1984): 2706–15.

Diagnostic Tests before Second-Look Laparotomy

The CA125 blood test, computed tomography (CT) scan, and Oncoscint scanning are three diagnostic tests that can be performed before second-look laparotomy. While none is as accurate as second-look surgery in detecting persistent ovarian cancer, they can give some indication whether there is any benefit to having the procedure.

Of those women with CA125 levels elevated above normal limits at the completion of their prescribed chemotherapy, 95 percent will be found to have persistent ovarian cancer at second-look laparotomy. Some health-care professionals would argue that these women are not candidates for the procedure. Fifty percent of women with normal CA125 levels will be found to have persistent ovarian cancer at second-look laparotomy. To reduce these false negative CA125 results, researchers at Duke University evaluated another blood cancer antigen, OVXI. They found that one-third of the women with normal CA125 results and persistent ovarian cancer also had elevated OVXI levels.

CT scans of the pelvis and abdomen are somewhat effective in detecting tumors larger than $3/4$ of an inch (2 cm), but are not sensitive enough to detect tumors $3/8$ of an inch (1 cm) or smaller.

Another method of detecting the presence of tumor deposits in the pelvis and abdomen uses Oncoscint, an indium (a silvery metallic element)-labeled antibody. Oncoscint is picked up by adenocarcinoma cells after injection into a vein and then the pelvis and abdomen are scanned in a manner similar to using a Geiger counter.

What Does Second-Look Laparotomy Involve?

The technique of second-look laparotomy is similar to that of meticulous surgical staging for early-staged ovarian cancer (chapter 7). The diaphragm is evaluated, any residual omentum is removed, pelvic and aortic lymph nodes are removed (if they have not been sampled at the original operation), and an abdominal wash is done. In addition, all suspicious areas are sampled and all confirmed tumor locations are rebiopsied, even if they appear normal.

If microscopic amounts of cancer are still present or the surgeon can remove the tumor deposits and leave only microscopic amounts of cancer, the patient may be a candidate for intraperitoneal chemotherapy (i.e., chemotherapy delivered directly into the peritoneal cavity), which may result in a remission and improved survival. You'll read more about intraperitoneal chemotherapy in chapter 10.

A Look at the Numbers

Today, the medical benefits of second-look laparotomy remain controversial in light of less than encouraging statistics. We know, for example, that if we treat one hundred women with chemotherapy for advanced-staged ovarian cancer, twenty-five women (25 percent) will have no cancer at second-look laparotomy. However, we also know that twelve to thirteen of these twenty-five women (50 percent) will have a recurrence of their cancer within the first five years. This leaves only twelve to thirteen women (12 to 13 percent) of the original one hundred who will have no evidence of ovarian cancer five years after their original chemotherapy.

Although these are averages and each woman is an individual, oncologists who believe that second-look surgery is not beneficial point to these numbers to support that belief. Hopefully, these results will improve in the next few years when the five-year impact of using the most effective known chemotherapy, taxol and Platinol® (chapter 8), is known.

A FINAL NOTE ON SECOND-LOOK SURGERY BY A MEDICAL ONCOLOGIST

This experience strongly suggests that it is not simply an attempt at secondary debulking that is important, but rather the successful removal of all macroscopic disease. An important corollary that directly follows this conclusion is that only surgeons who are prepared to make an aggressive, but realistic attempt at maximal secondary tumor debulking at second-look laparotomy should be performing this procedure.*

The use of second-look laparotomy remains controversial. However, women with advanced ovarian cancer, who have completed a prescribed course of chemotherapy, may benefit from knowing that there is no cancer remaining and that, if cancer is still present, additional therapy is now available to help eradicate the disease. This may be enough reason for them to go forward. The decision is difficult and must be made with understanding between the patient and her oncologist.

---

*M. Markham, "Second-Look Laparotomies in Ovarian Cancer: A Medical Oncologist's Perspective," *Journal of Cancer Research and Clinical Oncology* 119 (1993): 318–19.

Chapter 10

Second-Line Chemotherapy

Dear Mr. Wilder:

I read your *People* magazine story—I cried. I read Gilda's book a day later—I cried again.

I know what you are feeling, Mr. Wilder. I have those same pains. From Gilda's book, your relationship started and ended in almost exactly the same time frame as ours. Gilda was younger and so dearly wanted children. But both our ladies could be living today had a few *simple, routine, inexpensive* tests been made early on. The stomach pains? Gilda was able to cry out; Odetta pleaded with me at night to "rub my tummy, D—!" They thought my wife was constipated! GOD!

D. H.

"I was totally shattered. All that I had believed was undone. I became terribly depressed. I just wanted to sleep; I didn't want to talk to anybody. I just couldn't believe it. I was furious that the cancer was so insidious, that it had tricked me; that this journey wasn't over. I had to think about mortality again, that I would actually die from this disease. And cancer was controlling me, again. Here it was June and we were talking about more treatments till November. How could I believe that this series would work when I had believed so much that the other treatments would work? My friend with the ovarian cancer called and told me that her second-look surgery showed no sign of cancer. I was so jealous that I didn't know what to believe anymore. Everyone around me was so positive, saying, 'This is the best thing.' I didn't believe that. I didn't trust anybody. I didn't want to hear about it. I hated the world." (*It's Always Something,* p. 191)

Of course, Gilda was shattered. Why wouldn't she be? She had put all of her strength, will, and determination into beating the cancer. She had undergone major surgery, endured nine months of first-line chemotherapy and then second-look surgery. Now, she was being told that she essentially had to start over. This time, with something called *second-line chemotherapy.* I am sure she was asking herself the obvious question: How could second-line chemotherapy succeed where the other treatments had failed? Oncologists, then and now, are still searching for an equally obvious answer.

Unfortunately, like Gilda Radner, most women with advanced-stage ovarian cancer will have a recurrence of their disease and require second-line chemotherapy. The best opportunity to change this will be to develop better first-line chemotherapies to preclude the need for second-line treatments. Taxol and Platinol® may be the answer, but at this point, it's too early to know for sure. Taxol was never used on Gilda—she was a few years too early.

Let's take a look at what we do know about second-line chemotherapy.

SECOND-LINE CHEMOTHERAPY
AFTER PLATINOL® AND CYTOXAN

After the important 1976 report that Platinol® was an effective second-line chemotherapy after first-line treatment with Melphalan® or Cytoxan, researchers at the University of Indiana in 1979 reported on the effectiveness of Platinol® and Cytoxan, plus the antitumor antibiotic Adriamycin, as first-line chemotherapy in advanced ovarian cancer. This regimen—referred to as PAC chemotherapy—became the most widely used first-line chemotherapy worldwide. However, in spite of several large analyses showing a small percentage increase in survival when Adriamycin was added to Platinol® and Cytoxan, most oncologists were using only Platinol® and Cytoxan (PC) in women with advanced ovarian cancer, including Gilda Radner.

The success of second-line chemotherapy in women whose advanced-stage ovarian cancer recurs after first-line PAC or PC depends on there being a significant length of time (twelve to eighteen months) between the last course of chemotherapy and development of recurrence. Studies indicate that between 60 and 70 percent of these women achieve a second remission after retreatment with Platinol®.

About 30 percent of women who did not respond to first-line Platinol® respond to the new agent taxol as second-line chemotherapy. However, on average, these responses have been brief (six to eight months), with rare exceptions lasting from one to two years. Because of the low response to taxol alone as second-line chemotherapy, the short duration of the responses and the reported effectiveness of taxol and Platinol® as first-line chemotherapy, most women whose advanced ovarian cancer recurs after first-line PAC or PC chemotherapy will receive taxol and Platinol® second-line chemotherapy.

SECOND-LINE CHEMOTHERAPY AFTER FIRST-LINE TAXOL AND PLATINOL®

Because taxol and Platinol® chemotherapy is so new, investigators are only now researching what might be effective as second-line chemotherapy if first-line taxol and Platinol® fail. Most such therapies are considered experimental at this time, pending the outcome of larger studies now in progress.

ORAL AGENTS

When oral chemotherapeutic agents became available, researchers theorized that daily exposure of the cancer cells to drugs might have a different effect than monthly, intermittent intravenous treatments. In a 1995 University of Wisconsin study, thirty-three women whose cancers had become resistant first to Platinol®, then to taxol, were treated with the oral alkylating agent Hexamethylmelamine (Hexalin) daily for twenty-one days per month. Twenty percent of the women had a partial remission, that is, a remission greater than or equal to 50 percent reduction in the size of the tumors.

Oncologists from Vancouver, Canada, reported a 25 percent response rate in thirty-one women with Platinol®-resistant (they had not received taxol) cancers treated with Etoposide (VP-16), given fourteen of every twenty-one days. However, these responses lasted only from two to nine months.

Tamoxifen (Nolvodex) is an anti-estrogen commonly used to treat women with breast cancer. Most studies on its use in recurrent advanced ovarian cancer have reported response rates ranging from 0 and 15 percent. However, in a small study conducted in 1993 by the Mid-Atlantic Oncology program, a 17 percent response rate was reported using Tamoxifen in twenty-nine women with Platinol®-resistant tumors. Two responses exceeded five years and side effects were minimal. There are no reports on the use of Tamoxifen after first-line taxol and Platinol®.

INTRAVENOUS SECOND-LINE CHEMOTHERAPY

The antimetabolite (see chapter 8) Gemcitabine is an experimental drug being tested in women with progressive ovarian cancer. In a report from Denmark, forty-two women who had Platinol®-resistant ovarian cancer were treated with Gemcitabine. Eight (19 percent) achieved a partial remission which lasted an average of eight months.

Topotecan is a new drug which recently received FDA approval for the treatment of women with metastatic ovarian cancer, whose cancer has failed to respond to initial chemotherapy. It is sold under the name of Hycamtin.® Topotecan is the first of the new class of drugs that kill cancer cells by inhibiting the enzyme topoisomerase I which is essential in the replication of DNA, and thus essential for the growth of tumors. In reports to the FDA's Oncologic Drug Advisory Committee (ODAC) for approval of topotecan, researchers reported that in women with recurrent ovarian cancer after the first-line platinum chemotherapy randomly allocated to receive either topotecan or taxol, 20.5 percent had an objective response to topotecan as compared to 13.2 percent to taxol. Because of these and other reports, ODAC unanimously approved topotecan for patients with metastatic ovarian cancer after initial or subsequent chemotherapy. Topotecan is administered as a thirty-minute intravenous infusion (1.5 mg/m^2) daily for five days every three weeks. The main side effects reported were neutropenia (low white blood cell count), nausea, and vomiting. Topotecan appears to be a new and important drug for the treatment of ovarian cancer.

There are no data on the effectiveness of either of these experimental drugs as second-line chemotherapy after first-line taxol and Platinol®.

INTRAPERITONEAL SECOND-LINE CHEMOTHERAPY

Before taxol was shown to be effective second-line chemotherapy in women with advanced ovarian cancer, many women with persistent or recurrent ovarian cancer were treated by administering the drugs directly into the abdominal cavity—a process known as second-line intraperitoneal chemotherapy. This therapy appeared to be a good choice because ovarian cancer characteristically remains localized within the abdominal cavity. However, studies in experimental tumor models demonstrated that intraperitoneal chemotherapy drugs penetrate only about 1.5 mm into tumor nodules, limiting the effectiveness of this approach. But the chemical characteristics of Platinol® may counter this limitation. Platinol® is a large molecule (high molecular weight). Because of its size, there would be limited absorption of Platinol® into the circulation and higher concentrations of Platinol® could be maintained in the abdominal cavity. It is hoped that these higher doses of Platinol® would be more effective than the standard dose that can be safely administered intravenously.

In a 1994 study from Roswell Park Cancer Institute, sixty-three patients with recurrent or persistent ovarian cancer after a first-line Platinol® regime were given high-dose intraperitoneal Platinol® and Cytarabine as second-line chemotherapy. For those women with very small tumors—less than $\frac{1}{4}$ of an inch (5 cm)—at the time of intraperitoneal chemotherapy, over 40 percent survived five years.*

---

*See Appendix, Figure 2: "Evaluation of Survival . . ."

There are no results of intraperitoneal chemotherapy after first-line taxol and Platinol®.

HIGH-DOSE CHEMOTHERAPY WITH BONE MARROW TRANSPLANT

Just as severe bacterial infections become resistant to antibiotics, many ovarian cancers eventually become resistant to conventional chemotherapy. Although men and women with leukemia and lymphoma (cancer of the lymph nodes) may develop resistance to standard-dose chemotherapy, very high-dose chemotherapy (three to ten times the standard dose), followed by a reinfusion of the person's own normal bone marrow (autologous bone marrow transplant) several days after, has overcome this drug resistance and resulted in cures of these diseases. Similar data in other cancers are hard to come by, although many women with recurrent breast cancer after conventional chemotherapy are currently undergoing this procedure. To date, high-dose chemotherapy and bone marrow transplantation are only rarely performed in women with recurrent ovarian cancer. But the theory is, *the more chemotherapy the better.*

Here's how it works. The patient receives a general anesthetic. Bone marrow is removed from the iliac bone at the top of the hip area and frozen. High-dose chemotherapy is then given over a two- to five-day period in a specialized unit equipped with air filtration systems to lower the risk of infection. Several days later, the frozen bone marrow is thawed and reinfused (transplanted) intravenously to replenish the bone marrow supply destroyed by the high-dose chemotherapy. Recovery usually takes three to four weeks, but may be sooner if colony-stimulating factors (chapter 8) are used.

To date, fewer than two hundred cases of high-dose chemotherapy and bone marrow transplant for ovarian cancer have been reported in the medical literature. Most transplant centers have treated only between twenty and thirty cases. A *standard* treatment protocol for ovarian cancer is evolving. However, most centers using high-dose chemotherapy and bone marrow transplant report a very high response rate, ranging up to 75 percent, but only lasting between six and twelve months. In a 1994 report from Loyola University in Chicago, researchers reported on thirty women, twenty of whom had Platinol®-resistant tumors treated with high-dose Mitoxantrone, Carboplatin, and Cytoxan, followed by bone marrow transplant. Nearly 90 percent responded and 23 percent were alive without ovarian cancer at three years. Whether this procedure will be effective after first-line taxol and Platinol® is not known.

As we have learned, a new, effective drug for ovarian cancer comes along every ten to fifteen years: Melphalan® in the 1970s, Platinol® in the 1980s, and taxol in the 1990s. Until research gives us the final verdict on the value of taxol and Platinol® as first-line chemotherapy, high-dose chemotherapy and bone marrow transplant may be part of the answer to second-line chemotherapy in women with recurrent advanced ovarian cancer.

Now that we've examined the orthodox methods of surgery and chemotherapy, we should take a look at less conventional ways of dealing with ovarian cancer.

Chapter 11

Alternative Therapies from Apricot Pits to Zen Macrobiotic Diet and Touch Therapy

Dear Mr. Wilder:

I was touched by your article in *People* magazine on ovarian cancer. Gilda would have been proud of the way you have used your combined force of fame to not only achieve public awareness but the impossible task of going to Congress and informing them of the much-needed changes. If Gilda had been Miss Nobody and Gene had been a loving but quiet man, nothing would have been accomplished.

Obviously, Gilda's strength came from you and yours from her. Thank you for using it wisely. We all don't get an equal chance to change things that are wrong with society. Perhaps the haunting question of *Why me?* that always comes in tragedy can be answered for you now. No other couple could have accomplished what you did. Really!

M. J. B.

"... Then Gene and I had a huge fight because I said I wanted to go to Mexico and have laetrile treatments from apricot pits or something like that. Joanna [Bull] had sent

141

me a book called *Cancer Survivors* about alternative therapies outside of standard medical treatment. There are
about ten treatments described in the book, and of
course, after each one, I thought, *Well, I'm going to do
that!* So there was Gene, hoping we would have a normal
evening, eating dinner and watch a little TV. I turned to
him and said, 'Will you go to Mexico with me if I have this
laetrile?' (I just read that chapter in *Cancer Survivors.*)

"He flipped out. He had just had it. He said, 'No.
Absolutely not!'

"He said, 'I'm not going. No peach pits.' He smashed
his dinner plate on the floor. 'I'm not going and having you
do peach pits!'

"I yelled, 'Well, what if I'm dying and that was the last
resort?' " (*It's Always Something,* pp. 229–30)

How Gilda and Gene reacted at first to their seemingly devastating news is probably the norm, but most of us never
get to actually read or hear about it. As Suzy Kalter writes in her
book for those being treated for cancer, *Looking Up,* "With your
diagnosis, you cross over into a world that cannot be understood
by anyone who has not been in a life-threatening situation. Just
as no one can really understand what it is like for someone else
to have survived a concentration camp, a bombing, or the life of
extreme poverty and hardship, no one but another cancer sur-
vivor can understand your new position in life."*

Why wouldn't anyone turn to apricot pits, coffee enemas,
shark cartilage, or other "remedies" that promise a cure for cancer? Some patients want to understand what they are up against
in detail—statistics, tables, and figures—and this knowledge
gives them what they feel is more control over the situation. But
others are fearful of the details, even though they want to get better just as much as Gilda Radner, who once stated, *"Please, someone protect me from the cancer. Make me feel safe again."*

---

*Suzy Kalter, *Looking Up* (New York: McGraw Hill, 1987).

Since 1971, when President Richard M. Nixon's State of the Union Address included a declaration of war on cancer, the number of deaths from ovarian cancer has risen from 9,978 that year to 14,800 in 1996, an increase of 32 percent. There are many scientific and medical reasons for this grim statistic. However, given this fact, the fear and desperation of cancer patients often lead them to seek alternative therapies to standard medical therapy. With all the high technology now in use, many cancer patients fear that they don't have control of their own destiny. Sometimes, a single personal testimony on an alternative therapy heard on television or read in a magazine or tabloid newspaper has more personal meaning to many than a report of new cancer advances in the *New England Journal of Medicine*.

The actor and the cancer surgeon each consume a vitamin C and vitamin E tablet daily. We have no proof that these so-called *antioxidants* actually prevent cancer, but we have each read enough in the lay press to follow the philosophy, "It can't hurt and it might help." For people facing an advanced cancer, there is a more urgent desire to try methods that "might help, but can't hurt." This led, in part, to the use of Krebiozen in the 1960s; Laetrile in the 1970s; macrobiotic diets in the 1980s; and touch therapy, shark cartilage, relaxation therapy, and the like in the 1990s. It sounds similar to our discussions of Melphalan® in the 1970s, Platinol® in the 1980s, and taxol in the 1990s as the major advances in chemotherapy for ovarian cancer. For anyone reviewing the statistics of these three decades, which have improved the outcome for women with ovarian cancer but fall short of what we hoped for, it's not surprising that the development of new alternative therapies has paralleled that of standard medical therapies over the same period.

A report in the February 6, 1996, issue of *U.S. News & World Report* succinctly puts in perspective how far we have come in ovarian cancer relative to alternative therapies:

Jon Seskevich's hands hover over Kathleen Beil's abdomen, chest, throat and head. "I'm able to sense a disturbance in the energy field," he says. Using spiritual energy, Seskevich [a nurse clinician at Duke Comprehensive Cancer Center in Durham, North Carolina] tries to unruffle her field and so aid in the recovery of the fifty-three-year-old woman. Beil, who is recuperating from surgery for early ovarian cancer, says Seskevich's "healing touch" therapy makes her feel peaceful.

By one estimate, half of cancer patients turn to unorthodox treatments—from therapeutic touch to herbal treatments, to shark cartilage. But Beil, a homemaker from Durham, didn't seek out Seskevich's healing hands. Seskevich approached her, with the approval of her doctor, John Soper, during Beil's hospitalization for cancer surgery. "I think it's calming, if nothing else," says Soper, professor of Gynecologic Oncology. "You can convey a lot of reassurance by the old laying on of hands even if scientifically you can't prove the benefit."

When the war on cancer was first declared, it was improbable that Duke—or any mainstream hospital—would offer such treatment, conceded Dr. O. Michael Colvin, Duke's director. Some cancer patients treated conventionally at Duke also received guided imagery (patients imagine their tumors shrinking), meditation, biofeedback and prayer.

INJECTABLE ALTERNATIVE THERAPIES: KREBIOZEN, LAETRILE, ANTINEOPLASTON

Dr. Steven Durovic produced *Krebiozen* from a horse serum injected with the fungus *Actinomyces bovis*. Testing demonstrated that Krebiozen contained mineral oil and a form of creatinine, a waste product excreted from the kidneys. The medical charts of five hundred patients treated with Krebiozen were investigated by the National Cancer Institute, and Krebiozen was found to have no anticancer properties.*

Laetrile was first used as an injectable agent by E. T. Krebs in 1952. Laetrile represents a group of chemicals, the principal ingredient of which is amygdalin, which is derived from a variety of food products, including the pits of apricots, cherries, peaches, apples, and pears. Although it is not a vitamin, its producers referred to Laetrile as *vitamin* B-17. Some patients treated with Laetrile actually developed cyanide poisoning. Laetrile was studied by the National Cancer Institute in 178 patients, and was found to have no anticancer properties.

Although Dr. Stanislaw Burzynski was indicted in November 1995, following a U.S. Postal Service and FDA raid of his Houston clinic, he continues to treat cancer patients at his research institute in Houston with a product he calls *Antineoplaston*. Antineoplastons are a group of peptides originally isolated from urine. The theory is that these peptides are able to control tumor growth. A clinical trial by the National Cancer Institute was halted after only a small number of patients could be enrolled.†

ANTITOXIN THERAPY:
COFFEE ENEMAS, ZEN MACROBIOTIC DIET

The theory of *Antitoxin Therapy* is that inadequate elimination of colonic waste from the body interferes with metabolism, and that any method that *detoxifies* or purges the body of these toxins will prevent or treat cancer. Coffee enemas and diets high in fruit

---

*National Cancer Institute Cancer Net, "Unconventional Methods of Cancer Treatment. Krebiozen," January 1996.

†B. R. Cassileth and C. C. Chapman, "Alternative Therapy and Complimentary Cancer Therapies," *Cancer* 77 (1996): 1026–34.

and vegetables are used to achieve this. Gilda Radner used coffee enemas in an attempt to relieve her abdominal symptoms just one month before her diagnosis of stage IV ovarian cancer.

The *Macrobiotic Diet* forbids the use of red meat and animal products, and stimulants such as teas and coffee are to be used only sparingly. The diet consists largely of cereal products such as rice and wheat. The Zen philosophy, which is part of the macrobiotic diet, holds that meditation and adherence to the Zen diet counteract the two forces of *yin* and *yang*. *Yin* cancers (affecting the colon, stomach, and bladder) are caused by an excessive intake of *yin* foods—stimulants in alcohol, tea, and coffee; *yang* cancers (affecting the lungs and liver), by an excess of *yang* foods—red meat and smoked fish. Meditation is the other major vehicle to achieve balance between *yin* and *yang*.

Gilda Radner had become so obsessed with the macrobiotic diet that she purchased a gas stove for cooking because the electric models are prohibited. She consulted the best macrobiotic diet counselor. She occasionally ate at the Macrobiotic Center in New York. She wore only clothing made from cotton, discarding all of her clothes of other materials. She removed her rings, earrings, and all jewelry. She wore no nail polish and changed her cosmetics to natural products. She used herbal soaps, seaweed toothpaste. She hired a macrobiotic cook, who also spoke to her all the time about healing. She would not speak on the phone because the phone was draining her energy. No one, including Gene, could come near her while she ate. She tried to adopt an attitude of being humble and in touch with nature (her cook advised her to walk barefoot in the fresh dew on the grass before breakfast, and to plant a garden to be in touch with nature). While all this may sound bizarre, it indicates Gilda Radner's desperate efforts to get well by resorting to any means she thought might help her.

SHARK CARTILAGE

Shark Cartilage has become very popular since the book *Sharks Don't Get Cancer* by I. William Lang, Ph.D., was published in 1992. Enthusiasm for using shark cartilage was based on research that demonstrated that a protein in cartilage may inhibit tumor growth. The skeleton of a shark is entirely cartilage and, therefore, a good source of this protein. However, this protein in shark cartilage is not absorbed and is excreted. It is sold in health food stores to avoid clinical trials to prove its effectiveness and safety, and is therefore not FDA-approved. There is no evidence that shark cartilage is effective in treating cancer.

PSYCHOTHERAPY, COUNSELING, RELAXATION EXERCISES, VISUALIZATION, TOUCH THERAPY

There is no doubt that *psychotherapy, counseling,* and *relaxation exercises* can be very beneficial to any woman being treated for ovarian cancer. There is also no doubt that the love, support, and understanding of family and friends make the journey immeasurably easier. Sadly, some women with ovarian cancer seem to go the journey almost alone. *Visualization* techniques are used to help the patient visualize her defense system fighting against the cancer. All of these methods incorporate a healthy diet, exercise, and stress reduction.

Dr. O. Carl Simonton's book *Getting Well Again* includes a method of relaxation and imagery used along with standard medical treatment. This combination gives the patient a sense of control over her disease, improves her sense of well-being, and promotes relaxation. Dr. Simonton has not published any well-designed study of his results.

Unlike the science that we discussed in clinical trials for testing new drugs for ovarian cancer, scientific documentation for psychotherapy, counseling, relaxation exercises, and visualization is more difficult to come by; but it doesn't mean that they should not be used when combined with standard medical therapy.

It's clear that some patients *who want to get better* appear to do much better than those who don't, although we don't know why. However, it was unclear why some patients who received a placebo sugar tablet for pain relief achieved great relief, until we learned that the brain releases a morphine-like substance into the circulation in response to the placebo tablet. We still have much to learn about psychotherapy, relaxation exercises, and visualization.

As reported in *U.S. News & World Report, touch therapy* is being used in many major hospitals in the United States. The therapist does not actually touch the patient, but his/her arms move around the patient with the idea of smoothing out the energy field surrounding the patient. The patient cannot detect the energy field; only the therapist can.

A FINAL NOTE ON ALTERNATIVE THERAPIES

In 1992, Congress established the Office of Alternative Medicine within the National Institutes of Health to study alternative therapies. Although it has a very small budget, the fact that it is part of the federal government has lent a degree of respectability to these therapies. Any individual fighting a life-threatening illness, such as ovarian cancer, needs all the emotional and psychological support available. Methods of stress reduction are essential to this emotional and psychological well-being. "Alternative methods" would be better described as "complimentary therapy" (to conventional medicine), since, although scientific progress in treating women with ovarian cancer is always too slow for the person being treated, the progress made to date is still the best we have for prolonging and improving her quality of life. Complimentary therapy that helps in this battle can only be applauded; but it must never be a substitute.

Chapter 12

Gene Therapy

Dear Dr. Piver:
 I'd like to say that I think all the work that Gene Wilder has done is terrific. Gilda would surely be pleased.

K. L. S.

This final chapter begins with a look at what someday soon may be a new chapter for women with ovarian cancer—gene therapy.

As we've learned, ovarian cancer results from cumulative defects (mutations) in the genes of the cells that make up the ovary. Some of these defects can be inherited. Most genetic defects in ovarian cancer occur as a secondary event to an environmental factor or factors acting on the cells of the ovary. You'll recall, hopefully, that the American high-fat diet, fertility-stimulating drugs, talc powder, and the repeated trauma to the ovaries of never having been pregnant are some of these factors. Given that ovarian cancer is essentially a disease caused by gene defects, two questions arise: Can these gene defects be repaired? And, if so, will this repair result in a cure for women with ovarian cancer?

150

Advances in genetic engineering have given researchers the tools that may be able to correct or modify hereditary suscepti- bility to cancer by transplanting normal copies of genes into cells that have defective copies of those genes. These tools may also make it possible to deliver chemotherapy directly to the tumor, and to make tumors more sensitive to chemotherapy, while at the same time less likely to develop resistance.

While gene therapy has been shown to be theoretically feasible and exciting, its practical applications and implications for cure are still evolving. In fact, the first studies at the National Cancer Institute were performed in 1989. These studies found that gene therapy could be used safely. Since then, over a hundred clinical trials have been designed to evaluate the safety, side effects, and clinical bene- fits of gene therapy.

To give just one example, researchers at Tulane University and the University of Rochester are using gene therapy to treat women who have not responded to Platinol® chemotherapy and who have recurrent tumors smaller than $\frac{5}{8}$ of an inch (2 cm).* In their study, ovarian cancer cells from another patient are grown in culture and infected with the Herpes simplex (cold sore) virus. It is proposed that these altered ovarian cancer cells—now sensitive to antiviral agents—are carried into the recipient's ovarian cancer cells in the abdominal cavity by the Herpes simplex virus and will be destroyed by a seven-day course of the antiviral agent Ganciclovir. The gene therapy is repeated twice over a six-week period and then a second- look laparoscopy or laparotomy is performed to evaluate its effec- tiveness on recurrent ovarian tumors.

Results of this and other early studies are not available. It is clear that the final verdict on gene therapy for ovarian and other cancers is probably years away; but, if successful, it will be a new way of attacking the cancer cell without surgery, radiation, or chemotherapy.

---

*S. M. Freeman, C. McCume, W. Robinson, et al., "Clinical Protocol. The Treatment of Ovarian Cancer with a Gene-Modified Cancer Vaccine: A Phase I Study," *Gene Therapy* 6 (1995): 927–39.

SEMIFINAL THOUGHTS: PUBLIC INTEREST

There has been a noticeable decline in the intense public interest in ovarian cancer that gripped the nation following Gilda Radner's untimely death in May 1989. Prior to her death, ovarian cancer was referred to as the "silent killer" because there appeared to be no warning symptoms and because very few people spoke openly about the disease. Gilda Radner's death changed all that. Because of who she was, it became difficult to find someone who didn't want to talk or write about ovarian cancer.

At about that time, new discoveries that had not received much notice in the lay media—the use of the CA125 blood test, ultrasound in diagnosing ovarian cancer, and the fact that a woman could inherit the gene that causes ovarian cancer (as Gilda Radner did)—became topics of great interest. The "Oprah Winfrey" show, "Nightline," the "Today" show, Connie Chung, "20/20," "Dateline," CNN, "Good Morning America," the *New York Times, Washington Post, Los Angeles Times, Philadelphia Enquirer, Redbook, Self, Ms., Saavy, People, Chatelaine, Lears, Ladies Home Journal, Family Circle, Women's World, American Health, Good Housekeeping, McCalls,* and *Reader's Digest* all carried lead stories on ovarian cancer.

With the passage of time, however, this intense interest has begun to fade, especially as women have realized that breast cancer is taking almost three times as many lives as ovarian cancer. Thus the media has turned its attention to the number-two cancer killer of women, breast cancer. While this interest and media attention are appropriate and very important, the fact remains that the death rate from ovarian cancer has increased 32 percent since President Nixon declared war on cancer in 1971. Ovarian cancer should not be relegated to its former days of silence by the public or the media. It's too important.

Clearly, more effort is needed to deal with the ever-increasing death rate from ovarian cancer. Women can do something about the number-one cancer killer in women—lung cancer: they can quit smoking. They can have mammogram screenings for breast cancer. They can have sigmoidoscopy and colonoscopy for colon cancer, the number-three cancer killer. What is needed in the battle (the metaphor is considered appropriate) against ovarian cancer is an all-out effort for early detection and prevention similar in scope to the Manhattan Project in World War II or, more recently, the $20 million promised by former junk bond dealer and prostate cancer patient Michael Milken to a single researcher who can organize the best minds to find a cure for prostate cancer.

FINAL THOUGHTS

I wanted to end on an upbeat note. So, as I did almost daily, I sent a fax to Gene Wilder on January 31, 1996, asking for some "Gene therapy" in doing this. His reply of the same day says it all.

Dear Steve:

I would think that the best conclusion to this book would be a chapter on:

SO WHAT DO I DO?

I. If you already have been diagnosed with ovarian cancer:

Become a partner with your doctor on the plans for treatment and understanding what they involve. Not being a puppet or a soldier, following orders, but an actual partner. Your doctor does his or her part; you do your part. And if you don't understand—ask! (etc.)

Find a Gilda's Club or Wellness Community or any other reputable psychological/social support group in your community where there are other people in the same boat—a place where you can cry if you want to and express your frustration and laugh at some of the fears you had that you thought were peculiar to you alone.

When Gilda found out that there were fourteen other women in the room who felt guilty because they hadn't felt like sleeping with their husbands for weeks and weeks, they all laughed till they cried, and then came home and told their husbands that it wasn't their fault and that it was some temporary thing that usually happens.

II. Early Detection

The importance of early detection cannot be overstated. Although symptoms of ovarian cancer are often vague, they may be suggestive and should be checked out. If it is caught early, survival rates are very good. Women should know if they are at risk for ovarian cancer, especially if they have a family history of ovarian cancer. It is important to reemphasize that if a woman has a family history of ovarian cancer or is experiencing persistent symptoms, she should see her doctor and ask for the three tests that might help spot the problem early: a pelvic examination, sonogram of the ovary, and the blood test CA125. Although these tests are not foolproof, they are the best hope for early detection.

> Anyway, you might find this a starting
> point for the last chapter.
>
> LOVE,
> Your Sidekick

A good *starting point*, probably; a better *ending point*, certainly!

Appendix

Table 2.1

Ovarian Cancer & Milk Consumption:
Roswell Park Cancer Institute, 1982–1988

Ovarian Cancer (297) Controls (587)

Milk	Ovarian Cancer Risk
Skim	Decreased
Two Percent	Decreased
One Glass Whole Milk	None
More Than One Glass Whole Milk	Increased 3 Times

C. Mettlin and M. S. Piver, "A Case-Control Study of Milk Drinking and Ovarian Cancer Risk," *American Journal of Epidemiology* 132 (1990): 871–76.

This study demonstrates that drinking more than one glass of whole milk with its high fat content increased the risk of ovarian cancer as compared with skim milk, 2 percent, or one glass of whole milk.

Table 2.2

Ovarian Cancer & Consumption of Dairy Products
(The Harvard Study)

Monthly or Greater Consumption	Ovarian Cancer (235 total)	Controls (239 total)
Dairy Product	Ovarian Cancer Risk	Increased Risk
Yogurt (226 gm)	YES	1.7 times
Cottage Cheese (113 mg)	YES	1.4 times
Ice Cream (113 gm)	NO	
Ice Milk (236 ml)	NO	
Skimmed Milk (236 ml)	NO	
Whole Milk (236 ml)	NO	

D. W. Cramer, "Galactose Consumption and Metabolism in Relation to the Risk of Ovarian Cancer," *Lancet* 2 (1989): 66–71.

This study reiterated that eating large amounts of yogurt and cottage cheese slightly increased the risk of developing ovarian cancer.

Table 2.3

Ovarian Cancer & Talc Exposure in Perineal Hygiene
(The Harvard Study)

	Ovarian Cancer (215 total) Controls (215 total)
Exposure	Increased Ovarian Cancer Risk
No talc	None
Talc on sanitary pads or dusting powder	1.9 times

D. W. Cramer et al., "Ovarian Cancer and Talc," *Cancer* 50 (1982): 372–76.

This study demonstrated that using talc on sanitary pads or dusting powder as compared to never using talc nearly doubled the risk of developing ovarian cancer.

Table 2.4

Ovarian Cancer & Risk of Unprotected Intercourse
(Stanford University Study)

Years of Unprotected Intercourse	Increased Ovarian Cancer Risk
Less than 2	None
Between 2 and 9	1.5 times
10 or more	1.8 times

Adapted from A. S. Whittemore, M. L. Wu, R. S. Paffenbarger, et al., "Epithelial Ovarian Cancer and the Ability to Conceive," *Cancer Research* 49 (1989): 4047.

This study demonstrated that women who had unprotected intercourse for ten or more years and had never become pregnant nearly doubled their risk for developing ovarian cancer.

Table 2.5

Ovarian Cancer & Use of Fertility Drugs
(Women Who Had Been Pregnant Plus Those Who Had Not)
Collaborative Ovarian Cancer Group Study

Fertility Drug Use	Ovarian Cancer Cases	Controls	Increased Risk*
No	76	124	None
Yes	20	11	2.8 times
TOTAL	96	135	

Odds Ratio

A. S. Whittemore et al., "Characteristics Relating to Ovarian Cancer Risk: Collaborative Analysis of 12 U.S. Case-Control Studies. II. Invasive Epithelial Ovarian Cancer in White Women," *American Journal of Epidemiology* 136 (1992): 1184–1203.

This study showed that women who took fertility drugs, as compared to those who did not, nearly tripled their risk for developing ovarian cancer.

Table 2.6

**Ovarian Cancer & Use of the Fertility Drug Clomid
Seattle, Washington, Study**

	Ovarian Cancer Cases (11)	Controls (135)	Increased Risk
No Clomid	2	48	None
Yes Clomid	9	87	2.2 times
Clomid 1–11 cycles	3	74	None
Clomid 12 or more cycles	5	18	7.2 times

Number of cycles of Clomid unknown for one case of ovarian cancer and five controls.

M. A. Rossing et al., "Ovarian Tumors in a Cohort of Infertile Women," *New England Journal of Medicine* 33 (1994): 771–76.

This study demonstrated that women who took Clomid for more than twelve monthly cycles increased their risk for ovarian cancer over seven times.

Table 3.1

Oral Contraceptive Use & Decreased Risk of Ovarian Cancer Cancer and Steroid Hormone Study Group

Ovarian Cancer Cases (439)   Controls (3,867)

Duration of Use	Decreased Ovarian Cancer Risk
3–6 months	40%
7–11 months	30%
1–2 years	30%
3–4 years	40%
5–9 years	60%
10 years or more	80%

"The Reduction in Risk of Ovarian Cancer Associated with Oral Contraceptives. Cancer and Steroid Hormone Study," *New England Journal of Medicine* 316 (1987): 650–55.

This study demonstrates that the longer one takes oral contraceptives, the greater the reduction in the changes of developing ovarian cancer.

Table 3.2

Pregnancy & Decreased Risk of Ovarian Cancer
Collaborative Ovarian Cancer Group Study

Ovarian Cancer Cases (1,363)   Controls (5,609)

Number of Full-Term Pregnancies	Decreased Ovarian Cancer Risk*
0	0%
1	40%
2	47%
3	52%
4	64%
5	67%
6 or more	71%
Any term pregnancy	53%

Odds ratio

A. S. Whittemore et al., "Characteristics Relating to Ovarian Cancer Risk: Collaborative Analysis of 12 U.S. Case Control Studies," *American Journal of Epidemiology* 136 (1992): 1184–1203.

According to this study, the more full-term pregnancies a woman has, the greater the reduction in her chances of developing ovarian cancer.

Figure 3.3

Breast Feeding & Decreased Risk of Ovarian Cancer
Cancer and Steroid Hormone Study Group

Months of Breast Feeding	Decreased Ovarian Cancer Risk*
None	0%
1–2	40%
3–5	20%
6–11	20%
12–23	30%
24 or more	70%

Relative Risk

M. L. Gwinn et al., "Pregnancy, Breast Feeding, and Oral Contraceptives and the Risk of Epithelial Ovarian Cancer," *Journal of Clinical Epidemiology* 43 (1992): 559–62.

This study shows that the longer a woman breast feeds, the fewer the chances of her developing ovarian cancer.

Table 3.4

Tubal Ligation & Decreased Risk of Ovarian Cancer
The Nurses Health Study: 1976–1988

Tubal Ligation	Ovarian Cancer Cases (157)	Decreased Ovarian Cancer Risk*
No	148	
Yes	9	71%

Age adjusted relative risk

S. E. Hankinson et al., "Tubal Ligation, Hysterectomy and Risk of Ovarian Cancer," *Journal of the American Medical Association* 270 (1993): 2813–18.

A 71 percent decrease in the risk of ovarian cancer was observed for women who underwent tubal ligation as compared to those who did not.

Table 4.1

Symptoms of Early Localized and Nonlocalized
Advanced Ovarian Cancer

	Tumor Stage	
Main Symptom	Localized, I-IIA (172 patients)	Nonlocalized, IIB-IV (190 patients)
Abdominal Swelling	26.8%	24.3%
Abdominal Pain	16.9%	10.6%
Intestinal Symptoms	14.5%	24.2%
Vaginal Bleeding or Discharge	12.2%	11.6%
Burning on Urination	9.9%	4.7%
Fatigue and/or Fever	4.1%	14.6%
Tenesmus*	1.8%	—
Mammary Swelling	1.8%	—
Difficulty Breathing and/or Back Pain	1.8%	7.9%
No Symptoms	10.2%	2.1%

A painful spasm of the anal sphincter with an urgent desire to evacuate the bowel or bladder.

F. Flam, N. Einhorn, and K. Sjovall, "Symptomatology of Ovarian Cancer," *European Journal of Obstetrics and Gynecology Reproductive Biology* 27 (1988): 53–57.

This study demonstrates that women with localized stage I and stage II ovarian cancer have symptoms similar to those with more advanced stage IIB–IV ovarian cancer.

Table 4.2

CA125 Levels Higher Than 35 U/ml in Cancer

Cancer	Patients	% Elevated
Ovarian Carcinoma (by FIGO Stage)		
Stage I	254	41
Stage II	90	85
Stage III	529	93
Stage IV	169	97
All Stages	1,042	80
Ovarian Carcinoma (by Pathology)		
Serous	749	93
Undifferentiated	140	93
Endometrioid	130	85
Clear Cell	43	67
Mucinous	173	58
Ovarian Germ Cell Tumor	21	70
Ovarian Sex Cord Stromal Tumor	19	69
Borderline Tumor of the Ovary	50	56
Other Carcinomas		
Fallopian Tube	23	74
Pancreas	51	67
Liver	52	60
Lung	115	33
Cervix	506	29
Vulva	8	25
Endometrium	746	23
Breast	181	14
Colorectal	381	14
Stomach	105	13

Adapted from P. Kenemans et al., "CA125 in Gynecological Pathology–A Review," *European Journal of Obstetrics and Gynecology and Reproductive Biology* 49 (1993): 115–24.

This table demonstrates the percentage of women with elevated CA125 levels versus the stage of ovarian cancer, the type of ovarian cancer, and its elevation in other malignancies.

Table 4.3

CA125 Levels and Response to Therapy for Ovarian Cancer

Partial or Complete Remission			Progression of Disease		
Ovarian Cancer Cases	Falling CA125*	%	Ovarian Cancer Cases	Rising CA125	%
216	209	97	205	171	83

Significant rise or decrease in CA125 defined as at least doubling (progression) or halving (remission) compared to baseline values.

Adapted from P. Kenemans et al., "CA125 in Gynecological Pathology–A Review," *European Journal of Obstetrics and Gynecology and Reproductive Biology* 49 (1993): 115–24.

It is shown by this study that falling CA125 levels in women who have been treated for ovarian cancer correlates 97 percent of the time with response to therapy. For women whose ovarian cancer progresses during therapy, a rising CA 125 correlates with progression of the cancer 83 percent of the time.

Table 4.4

Transvaginal Color Flow Doppler in Differentiating Benign from Malignant Ovarian Tumors

Resistance to Blood Flow Resistance Index (RI)	Malignant Tumors	Benign Tumors
Low Resistance to Blood Flow RI < 0.40	96% (54)	0.16% (1)
Normal Resistance to Blood Flow RI > 0.40	4% (2)	98.4% (623)
TOTAL	100% (56)	100% (624)

Adapted from A. Kurjak, "Evaluation of Adnexal Masses with Transvaginal Color Ultrasound," *Journal of Ultrasound Medicine* 10 (1993): 295–97.

Malignant ovarian tumors have a low resistance to blood flow on color flow doppler imaging, whereas women with benign ovarian tumors have a normal resistance to blood flow 98 percent of the time.

Table 5.1

Common Epithelial Ovarian Cancers

I.   SEROUS CANCERS
   A. Serous carcinoma of low malignant potential (of borderline malignancy)
   B. Serous carcinoma

II. MUCINOUS CANCERS
   A. Mucinous carcinoma of low malignant potential (of borderline malignancy)
   B. Mucinous carcinoma

III. ENDOMETRIOID CANCERS
   A. Endometrioid carcinoma of low malignant potential (of borderline malignancy)
   B. Endometrioid carcinoma

IV. CLEAR CELL CANCERS
   A. Clear cell carcinoma of low malignant potential (of borderline malignancy)
   B. Clear cell carcinoma

V.   BRENNER CANCERS
   A. Brenner carcinoma of low malignant potential (of borderline malignancy)
   B. Brenner carcinoma

VI. UNDIFFERENTIATED CARCINOMAS
   A. Carcinomas not otherwise classifiable

Table 6.1

International Federation of Gynecologists and Obstetricians (FIGO) 1986 Staging for Ovarian Cancer

Stage	Characteristic
I	Growth limited to the ovaries.
IA	Growth limited to one ovary; no ascites (fluid in abdomen); no tumor on external surface, capsule intact
IB	Growth limited to both ovaries; no ascites; no tumor on external surface, capsule intact
IC	Tumor either stage IA or stage IB but with tumor on the surface of one or both ovaries, or with capsule ruptured, or with ascites containing malignant cells with positive peritoneal washings
II	Growth involving one or both ovaries on pelvic extension
IIA	Extension or metastases (spread) to the uterus or tubes
IIB	Extension to other pelvic tissues
IIC	Tumor either stage IIA or stage IIB but with tumor on the surface of one or both ovaries, or with capsule(s) ruptured, or with ascites containing malignant cells or with positive peritoneal washings
III	Tumor involving one or both ovaries with peritoneal implants outside the pelvis or positive retroperitoneal or inguinal nodes; superficial liver metastases equals stage III, tumor is limited to the true pelvis but with histologically verified malignant extension to small bowel or omentum
IIIA	Tumor grossly limited to the true pelvis with negative nodes but with histologically confirmed microscopic seeding of abdominal peritoneal surfaces
IIIB	Tumor of one or both ovaries; histologically confirmed implants of abdominal peritoneal surfaces, none exceeding 2 cm ($\frac{3}{4}$ of an inch) in diameter, nodes negative
IIIC	Abdominal implants greater than 2 cm ($\frac{3}{4}$ of an inch) in diameter, or positive retroperitoneal or inguinal nodes
IV	Growth involving one or both ovaries with distant metastases; if pleural effusion is present, there must be positive cytologic test results to allot a case to stage IV, parenchymal liver metastases equals stage IV

Table 7.1

Incidence of Occult or Microscopic Metastases in Apparent Stage I or II Ovarian Cancer

Sites of Occult or Microscopic Metastases	Stage I	Stage II
Diaphragm	11%	23.0%
Omentum	3%	7.0%
Paraaortic Lymph Nodes	13%	10.0%
Pelvic Lymph Nodes	8%	—
Abdominal "Wash"	33%	12.5%

M. S. Piver, J. J. Barlow, and S. B. Lele, "Incidence of Subclinical Metastasis in Stage I and II Ovarian Carcinoma," *Obstetrics and Gynecology* 52 (1978): 100.

This was the first collective study to demonstrate that women who were thought to have cancer limited to the ovary (stage I) or pelvis (stage II) had microscopic metastasis in one of these five sites.

Table 7.2

Surgery for Stage III and IV Ovarian Cancer

Surgery Performed	Percent
Hysterectomy	100
Ovarian Tumors	100
Omental Tumors	86
Abdominal Implants	40
Bowel Surgery	30
Rectum	16
Small Bowel	6
Large Bowel	6
Large Bowel and Colostomy	6
Large and Small Bowel	2
Appendix Tumor	10
Urinary Tract	6
Portion of Ureter	4
Portion of Bladder	2

M. S. Piver and T. R. Baker, "The Potential for Optimal ($\leq$ 2 cm) Cytoreductive Surgery in Advanced Ovarian Carcinoma at a Tertiary Medical Center: A Prospective Study," *Gynecologic Oncology* 24 (1986): 1–8.

This demonstrates the type of surgery required in a series of fifty consecutive women undergoing debulking surgery for ovarian cancer.

Figure 1

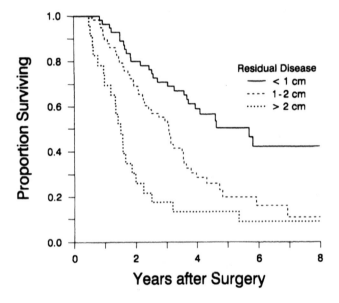

T. R. Baker, M. S. Piver, and R. E. Hempling, "Long-Term Survival by Cytoreductive Surgery to < 1 cm, Induction Weekly Cisplatin and Monthly Cisplatin, Doxorubicin, and Cyclophosphamide in Advanced Ovarian Adenocarcinoma," *Cancer* 74 (1994): 656–63. Copyright © 1994 by *Cancer.* Reprinted by permission of Wiley-Liss, a Division of John Wiley and Sons, Inc.

This study demonstrates that the best survival after debulking surgery and chemotherapy for advanced ovarian cancer is among those women who, after surgery, have residual tumor implants less than 1 cm (³⁄₈ of an inch).

Figure 2

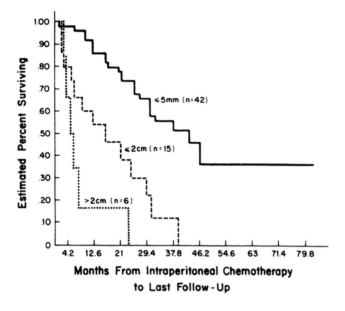

This study shows that patients with ≤5 mm residual tumor implants prior to second-line intraperitoneal chemotherapy achieve the longest long-term survival.

References and Bibliography

Chapter 2: Causes of Ovarian Cancer

Cramer, D. W. "Galactose Consumption and Metabolism in Relation to the Risk of Ovarian Cancer." *Lancet* 2 (1989): 66–71.

Cramer, D. W., et al. "Ovarian Cancer and Talc." *Cancer* 50 (1982): 372–76.

Kaspar, C. S., and Chandler, P. J. "Possible Morbidity in Women from Talc on Condoms." *JAMA* 273 (1995): 846–47.

Mettlin, C., and M. S. Piver. "A Case-Control Study of Milk Drinking and Ovarian Cancer Risk." *American Journal of Epidemiology* 132 (1990): 871–76.

Piver, M. S. "Prophylactic Oophorectomy and Ovarian Cancer Mortality." In *Cancer Prevention Series 1993*, V. T DeVita, Jr., S. Hellman, and S. A. Rosenberg, eds. Philadelphia: J. B. Lippincott Company, 1992, pp. 1–10.

Risch, H. A., et al. "Dietary Lactose Intake, Lactose Intolerance, and the Risk of Epithelial Cancer in Southern Ontario (Canada)." *Cancer, Causes and Control* 5 (1994): 540–48.

Rodriguez, C. "Estrogen Replacement Therapy and Fatal Ovarian Cancer." *American Journal of Epidemiology* 141 (1995): 828–35.

Rossing, M. A., et al. "Ovarian Tumors in a Cohort of Infertile Women." *New England Journal of Medicine* 33 (1994): 771–76.

Whittemore, A. S., et al. "Characteristics Related to Ovarian Cancer Risk: Collaborative Analysis of 12 U.S. Case-Control Studies. II. Invasive Epithelial Ovarian Cancer in White Women." *American Journal of Epidemiology* 136 (1992): 1184–1203.

Whittemore, A. S.; Wu, W. L.; Paffenbarger, R. S.; et al. "Epithelial Ovarian Cancer and the Ability to Conceive." *Cancer Research* 49 (1989): 4047.

Whittemore, A. S., et al. "Personal and Environmental Characteristics Related to Epithelial Ovarian Cancer. II. Exposure to Talcum Powder, Tobacco, Alcohol and Coffee." *American Journal of Epidemiology* 128 (1988): 1228–40.

Chapter 3: Prevention of Ovarian Cancer

Gross, T. P., and Schlesselman, J. J. "The Estimated Effect of Oral Contraceptive Use on the Cumulative Risk of Epithelial Ovarian Cancer." *Obstetrics and Gynecology* 83 (1994): 419–24.

Gwinn, M. L., et al. "Pregnancy, Breast Feeding, and Oral Contraceptives and the Risk of Epithelial Ovarian Cancer." *Journal of Clinical Epidemiology* 43 (1992): 559–62.

Hankinson, S. E., et al. "Tubal Ligation, Hysterectomy and Risk of Ovarian Cancer." *Journal of the American Medical Association* 270 (1993): 2813–18.

"The Reduction in Risk of Ovarian Cancer Associated with Oral Contraceptives. Cancer and Steroid Hormone Group Study." *New England Journal of Medicine* 316 (1987): 650–55.

Risch, H. A., et al. "Parity, Contraception and Infertility and the Risk of Epithelial Ovarian Cancer." *American Journal of Epidemiology* 140 (1994): 585–97.

Rosenblatt, K. A., et al. "Lactation and the Risk of Epithelial Ovarian Cancer." *International Journal of Epidemiology* 22 (1993): 192–97.

Whittemore, A. S., et al. "Characteristics Relating to Ovarian Cancer Risk: Collaborative Analysis of 12 U.S. Case-Control Studies." *American Journal of Epidemiology* 136 (1992): 1184–1203.

Chapter 4: Diagnosing Ovarian Cancer

Flam, F., et al. *European Journal of Obstetrics and Gynecology Reproductive Biology* 27 (1988): 53–57.

Kenemans, P., et al. "CA125 in Gynecological Pathology–A Review." *European Journal of Obstetrics and Gynecology Reproductive Biology* 49 (1993): 115–24.

Kurjak, A. "Evaluation of Adnexal Masses with Transvaginal Color Ultrasound." *Journal of Ultrasound Medicine* 10 (1991): 295–97.

Chapter 5: The Thirty Different Types of Ovarian Cancer: The Pathology of Ovarian Cancer

Piver, M. S., ed. *Ovarian Malignancies: Diagnostic and Therapeutic Advances.* London: Churchill Livingston, 1987.

Chapter 7: Surgery of Ovarian Cancer: What Do I Need to Know?

Baker, T. R.; Piver, M. S.; and Hempling, R. E. "Long-Term Survival by Cytoreductive Surgery to < 1 cm, Induction Weekly Cisplatin and Monthly Cisplatin, Doxorubicin, and Cyclophosphamide in Advanced Ovarian Adenocarcinoma." *Cancer* 74 (1994): 656–63.

Buchsbaum, H. J.; Brady, M. F.; Delgado, G.; et al. "Surgical Staging of Carcinoma of the Ovary." *Surgery Gynecology and Obstetrics* 169 (1989): 226.

Griffiths, C. T., and Fuller, A. F. "Intensive Surgical and Chemotherapeutic Management of Advanced Ovarian Cancer." *Surgical Clinics of North America* 58 (1978): 131–42.

Piver, M. S., and Baker, T. R. "The Potential for Optimal (≤ 2 cm) Cytoreductive Surgery in Advanced Ovarian Carcinoma at a Tertiary Medical Center: A Prospective Study." *Gynecologic Oncology* 24 (1986): 1–8.

Piver, M. S.; Barlow, J. J.; and Lele, S. B. "Incidence of Subclinical

Metastasis in Stage I and II Ovarian Carcinoma." *Obstetrics and Gynecology* 52 (1978): 100.

Scott, N. A., and Schofield, P. F. "Cytoreductive Surgery for Ovarian Carcinoma." *British Journal of Surgery* 77 (1990): 481–82.

Young, R. C.; Decker, D. G.; Wharton, J. T.; Piver, M. S.; Sindelar, W. F.; Edwards, B. K.; and Smith, J. P. "Staging Laparotomy in Early Ovarian Cancer." *Journal of the American Medical Association* 250 (1983): 3072–76.

Chapter 8: First-Line Chemotherapy of Ovarian Cancer

Bolis, G.; Colombo, N.; Pecorelli, S.; et al. "Adjuvant Treatment for Early Epithelial Ovarian Cancer. Results of Two Randomised Clinical Trials Comparing Cisplatin to No Further Treatment or Chromic Phosphate (P32)." *Annals of Oncology* 6 (1995): 887–94.

McGuire, W. P.; Hoskins, W. J.; Brady, M. F.; et al. "Cyclophosphamide and Cisplatin Compared with Paclitaxel and Cisplatin in Patients with Stage III and Stage IV Ovarian Cancer." *New England Journal of Medicine* 334 (1996): 1–6.

Young, R. C.; Walton, L. A.; Ellenberg, S. S.; et al. "Adjuvant Therapy for Stage I and II Epithelial Ovarian Cancer. Results of Two Prospective Randomised Trials." *New England Journal of Medicine* 322 (1990): 1021–27.

Chapter 9: Second-Look Surgery

Hoskins, W. J.; Rubin, S. C.; Dulaney, E.; et al. "Influence of Secondary Cytoreduction at the Time of Second-Look Laparotomy on the Survival of Patients with Epithelial Ovarian Carcinoma." *Gynecologic Oncology* 34 (1989): 365.

Markham, M. "Second-Look Laparotomies in Ovarian Cancer: A Medical Oncologist's Perspective." *Journal of Cancer Research and Clinical Oncology* 119 (1993): 318–19.

Piver, M. S. "Ovarian Carcinoma: A Decade of Progress." *Cancer* 54 (1984): 2706–15.

Surwit, E. A.; Childers, J. M.; Craig, D. N.; et al. "Clinical Assessment of 111Cyt-103 Immunoscintigraphy in Ovarian Cancer." *Gynecologic Oncology* 48 (1993): 287.

Walton, L.; Ellenberg, S. S.; Major, F.; et al. "Results of Second-Look Laparotomy in Patients with Early-Staged Ovarian Carcinoma." *Obstetrics and Gynecology* 70 (1987): 770.

Xu, F. J.; Yu, Y. H.; Daly, L.; et al. "OVXI Radioimmunoassay Compliments CA125 in Predicting Presence of Residual Ovarian Carcinoma at Second-Look Surgical Surveillance Procedure." *Journal of Clinical Oncology* 11 (1993): 1506.

Chapter 10: Second-Line Chemotherapy

Ahlgren, J. D.; Ellison, N. M.; Gottlieb, R. J.; et al. "Hormonal Palliation of Chemoresistant Ovarian Cancer: Three Consecutive Phase II Trials of the Mid-Atlantic Oncology Program." *Journal of Clinical Oncology* 11 (1993): 1957–68.

Hoskins, P. J., and Swenerton, K. D. "Oral Etoposide Is Active against Platinum-Resistant Epithelial Ovarian Cancer." *Journal of Clinical Oncology* 12 (1994): 60–63.

Kudel, K. A.; Andrzei, J.; Tresukosi, D.; Edwards, C. L.; et al. "Phase II Study of Intravenous Topotecan as a Five-Day Infusion for Refractory Epithelial Ovarian Carcinoma." *Journal of Clinical Oncology* 19 (1996): 1552–57.

Lund, B.; Hansen, O. P.; Theilade, K.; et al. "Phase II Study of Gemcitabine (2',2'-Difluorodeoxycytidine) in Previously Treated Ovarian Cancer Patients." *Journal of the National Cancer Institute* 86 (1994): 1530–33.

Markmam, M. "Second-Look Laparotomies in Ovarian Cancer: A Medical Oncologist's Perspective." *Journal of Cancer Research and Clinical Oncology* 119 (1993): 318–19.

Piver, M. S. "Ovarian Carcinoma: A Decade of Progress." *Cancer* 54 (1984): 2706–15.

Piver, M. S.; Recio, F. O.; Baker, T. R.; and Driscoll, D. "Evaluation of Survival after Second-Line Intraperitoneal Cisplatin-Based Chemotherapy for Advanced Ovarian Cancer." *Cancer* 73 (1994): 1693–98.

Schink, J. C.; Harris, L. S.; Grosen, E. R.; et al. "Altretamine (Hexalen) an Effective Salvage Chemotherapy after Paclitaxel (Taxol) in Women with Recurrent Platinum Resistant Ovarian Cancer." *Proceedings of the American Society of Clinical Oncology* 14, no. 770 (1985): 275.

Segna, R. A.; Dottino, P. R.; Mandeli, J. P.; et al. "Secondary Cytoreduction for Ovarian Cancer Following Cisplatin Therapy. *Journal of Clinical Oncology* 11 (1993): 434–39.

Shpall, E. J.; Jones, R. B.; Bearman, S. I.; et al. "Future Strategies for the Treatment of Advanced Epithelial Ovarian Cancer Using High-Dose Chemotherapy and Autologous Bone Marrow Support." *Gynecologic Oncology* 54 (1994): 357–61.

Stiff, P.; Bayer, R.; Camarda, M.; et al. "A Phase II Trial of High-Dose Mitoxantrone, Carboplatin, and Cyclophosphamide with Autologous Bone Marrow Rescue for Recurrent Epithelial Ovarian Carcinoma: Analysis of Risk Factors for Clinical Outcome." *Gynecologic Oncology* 57 (1995): 278–85.

Chapter 11: Alternative Therapies from Apricot Pits to Zen Macrobiotic Diet and Touch Therapy

American Cancer Society. *Shark Cartilage Angiogenesis.* Atlanta: American Cancer Society, 1992 report no. 81000.

Cassileth, B. R., and Chapman, C. C. "Alternative Therapy and Complimentary Cancer Therapies." *Cancer* 77 (1996): 1026–34.

Folkman, J. "The Role of Angiogenesis in Tumor Growth." *Seminars in Cancer Biology* 3 (1992): 65–71.

Kalter, Suzy. *Looking Up.* New York: McGraw Hill, 1987.

Lang, I. William. *Sharks Don't Get Cancer.* Garden City Park, N.Y.: Avery Publishing Group Inc., 1992.

National Cancer Institute Cancer Net. "Unconventional Methods of Cancer Treatment. Krebiozen." January 1996.

Simonton, O. Carl. *Getting Well Again.* Los Angeles: J. P. Tarcher, Inc., 1978.

"The War on Cancer." *U.S. News & World Report,* February 5, 1996, p. 71.

Chapter 12: Gene Therapy

Freeman, S. M.; McCune, C.; Robinson, W.; et al. "Clinical Protocol. The Treatment of Ovarian Cancer with a Gene-Modified Cancer Vaccine: A Phase I Study." *Human Gene Therapy* 6 (1995): 927–39.

Parker, S. L.; Tong, T.; Bolden, S.; and Wingo, P. A. "Cancer Statistics 1996." *CA: A Cancer Journal for Clinicians* 46 (1996): 5–28.

Index

CPSIA information can be obtained
at www.ICGtesting.com
Printed in the USA
LVOW12s1313010217
522874LV00001B/57/P